A SCHOOL IN THE FORTIES

Weston-super-Mare Grammar Schools 1940-1949

ALEC KINGSMILL

Karanfil Press

First Published in Great Britain in 2005
by
Karanfil Press, PO Box 8529, Nottingham NG5 0AG

ISBN 0-9550611-0-5

Printed in Great Britain by
Adlard Print & Reprographics Ltd.,
Ruddington, Nottingham NG11 6HH
Tel: 0115 921 4863
www.adlardprint.com

ACKNOWLEDGEMENTS

Many people responded to my request for recollections and photographs. To varying extents, I have embraced their contributions, as well as some from elsewhere, into the narrative, and thus I am very indebted to them all. I have listed them below in the alphabetical order of their surnames at the time they were at the school, followed by their married surnames where appropriate. I have then added the years that they attended the school.

NAME	MARRIED NAME	DATES	NAME	MARRIED NAME	DATES
Don Andrews		1938-1943	Janet Lovell	Williams	1942-1949
Ivan Armstrong		1941-1946	Janet Lovell	Owen	1941-1948
Frank Ashby		1937-1943	Adrian Lunnon		1942-1949
Jill Bryant	Banwell	1943-1950	Ray Millard		1936-1941
Valerie Champion	Tucker	1942-1949	Jim Owen		1941-1948
Don Andrews	Finney	1941-1948	John Owen		1939-1941
Dave Edwards		1936-1941	Roy Peacock		1940-1947
Margaret England	Peacock	1941-1947	Roy Perry		1940-1947
Gus Fletcher		1940-1945	Derek Porter		1940-1948
Graeme Forrester		1940-1947	Mary Price	Armstrong	1941-1947
Michael Gates		1943-1948	Judy Price	Hodge	1945-1950
Terry Gilbert		1941-1946	Polly Price	Hurley	1943-1948
June Hale	Moore	1937-1942	Leonard Reeves		1941-1946
Marian Hale	Kingsmill	1941-1947	Trevor Rowsell		1939-1944
Don Andrews		1938-1944	Freda Star		1949-1951
Arthur Hiscocks		1941-1945	Mary Thomas	Ashley	1939-1945
Valerie Hitchins	Croft	1941-1945	Ken Tucker		1944-1945
Denis Hodge		1943-1950	Charles Usher		1940-1945
Jean Innes	Saunders	1943-1948	Graham Venn		1939-1945
Jeff Hynds		1946-1948	Paul Warren		1943-1950
Ted Johnson		1937-1941	Peter Weaver		1943-1948
Bryan Jones		1944-1946			
Margaret Lacey	Lunnon	1943-1949			

Additionally, the following past girl pupils made later contributions to supplement memories of the Girl's Staff. Along with the year that they took the School Certificate, they were, Jean Ashley (Cook) 1950, Ann Bray (Kinchin)1946, Jocelyn Brewer (Beaton) 1948, Bernice Brookman (Russell) 1946, Peggy Clarke (Wintle) 1942, June Edmonds (Adams) 1950, June Ganfield (Sen Sharma) 1951, Joy Pinton 1943, Rosemary Sampson (Hodges)1946, Maureen Shorney (1950), and Rosemary Taylor (Gauntlett) 1946.

I am also very much indebted to Mrs. Joyce Petchey , of Barking Abbey School, and Mrs. Pamela Starling , of Mitcham County School.

Most of the photographs come from my own collection or have been contributed by past members of the school.
I apologise to the few others whose photos I have used, but for which the passage of time has made the determination of that ownership impossible.

CONTENTS

PREFACE

I am unsure if this preface is by way of an explanation or by way of a justification. Maybe it's an apology.

In recent years, solely as a hobby, I have written a number of recollections about events and circumstances which occurred in my own life, mainly prior to the 1960s. However that activity has almost come to an end. On the basis of a sighting of a couple of those scribblings Jeff Hynds who had recently taken over the convenorship of the annual reunion of those who were at the Weston-super-Mare County Schools more than fifty years ago, suggested that I might have a go at a 1940s recollection of those schools. Perhaps unrealistically I said that I would. What follows is the result.

I contacted quite a number of people from both the girls' school and the boys' school and have incorporated nearly everything that I received which had a relevance to the theme. Aspects of people's later lives also emerged, most of which I read with great interest, but if the project was to remain manageable I decided, with just a few exceptions, to confine the narrative to that which occurred in the 1940s.

I have tried to produce a document that any researcher might produce, but the decade and the school itself were my decade, it was my school. To achieve a sort of thread I have delved into my own recollections more than might, in a perfect world, have been ideal. Thus some of the content does reflect my own personal experience of those times - well not in the girls' school of course, although I did eventually marry a girls' school pupil of that era.

A by-product of this orientation is that the story is not totally even handed. In chronological terms it more reflects the experiences of people who joined the school at the beginning of the 1940s and left anywhere between five and eight years later. The centre of gravity might be expressed in terms of those who took school certificate in 1945 or 1946. But I have incorporated everything that I have received from all the other age groups. I therefore hope that what follows reflects a fair story of the whole decade, of interest to anyone who was there in the 1940s, and perhaps, even beyond. I suppose some might see it as a contribution to a social history of the 1940s, a temptation that I haven't entirely resisted. All expressed opinions are very much my own save where they are clearly attributed to others.

But there are other biases built into the narrative. Those who have had sufficient interest to write something down tend to be those who enjoyed their school days at Weston. There will be others who felt it is all best forgotten so their views are not represented. Try as I might I could not unearth as much about the girls as I could about the boys, so there is a content bias there as well. Then you cannot really cover many of the personal realities of growing up and it is easy to make it sound all a bit too jolly and a bit too carefree. People surely argued with their parents, spots grew on places where you wished they hadn't, infatuations didn't always get the response that you hoped for, routines could be boring and air raids could be very frightening.

But we survived.

Alec Kingsmill,
Nottingham,
June 2005

1

THE SCHOOL

Weston-super-Mare County School for Boys and Girls had its origins in Nithsdale Road, in the southern part of the town, in 1922. The school then comprised ex-Army huts which had been previously used as part of a military hospital near Warminster, during the first World War. The headmaster at that time, Mr T. E. Lindfield, has recalled how the school 'grew in strength and numbers, while the huts slowly rotted and decayed'.

In 1935, the new school building was opened in Broadoak Road, about half a mile away with, for the first time, a rigorous policy of segregating boys and girls. The girls' school and the boys' school were indeed separate schools.

gymnasia, separate cloakrooms, two art rooms, and indeed two senior science labs, although these were readily accessible to both schools. Above those on the uppermost floor was the girls' geography room. Below the clock tower in this central block was the hall. This had the stage at the boys' end and the kitchens and the projector room at the girls' end. But what must have been the pride and joy of the segregationists, and of the school's designer, (although in truth it also had a very practical purpose) was a huge monolithic moveable wall which could cut the hall into two halves. However, it could be reined back to its lair between the two gymnasia, when not required. It must have weighed several tons. Positioned in its deployed position it looked most substantial, even permanent, but alas it wasn't entirely soundproof.

The new school in 1935

The building itself, which seemed designed from the outset to be part of this policy of segregation, set the physical and influenced the social aspects of life at the school throughout the nineteen-forties. It is the physical backdrop to these recollections.

It was a very handsome school. The photograph shows a school built around two quadrangles, boys to the left (the east end), girls to the right (the west end).There were five classrooms on each side of the quadrangle - ten classroom in all, to each school. The central block, although largely monolithic in structure also perpetuated the segregation. It housed two

It wasn't moved to its stored position all that often, for winding it back to its own garage was a very tedious process. The principal occasions that the wall was withdrawn were the annual Speech days, when one school was given the afternoon off, and the other school had the use of whole hall.

At one end - the school's west end - were the girls administrative offices, the staff and headmistress's accommodation and the domestic science and the physics and chemistry laboratories. At the east end were the comparable staff quarters for the boys' staff, along with the woodwork shop, and again the chemistry lab and the physics lab. By the standards of the day these laboratories and work rooms were very generously laid out and equipped. Beyond the east end was a separate enclave that encompassed the boiler house and the house of the caretaker and his wife - Mr. and Mrs. Sam Dowdell. For June Hale, who arrived as a pupil in 1937, the school was 'very modern, very light and airy, and was well equipped with a very good gymnasium, science laboratory, and a domestic science room with cookers, sewing machines, good working space and even a little flatlet at one end that was sometimes used as a sick room'.

A boys' classroom

Sadly however, it does seem that the grace and appearance of the school was at the cost of some rather fundamental design faults. The basic building material seemed to be cast reinforced reconstituted sand stone blocks, in parts on a brick core. However, the reinforcing bars seemed to be affected by the salt laden atmosphere, they rusted, expanded and cracked the blocks. By 1939, the tower was covered in scaffolding whilst liquid cement was poured between the 'brickwork and the stone work'. This could hardly have been anything other than to address a structural problem By the 1940s, window ledges were beginning to crack and fall away. In 1953, the north veranda was dismantled because it had become unsafe. Presumably all this eventually led to the demise of the building, in 1999. It was all in some contrast to the schools built in the late Victorian period which still appear to be carrying out a noble service. The classrooms were indeed full of daylight and no doubt their performance in a future war wasn't a design consideration. There was an 'open-air' movement in education circles about that time and maybe the design brief saw pupils being taught in an almost open air environment, with all the doors flung wide open. Certainly, the classrooms had full height, metal framed, single glazed, glass doors to form the bulk of both sides, with sloping glass 'northern lights' above. Their thermal performance must have been appalling and the eventual risk they presented in the event of an untimely bomb was, at least in retrospect, frightening. As pupils however I do not think that in those days we thought on those lines. To address the situation presented by the fully opening side walls, the main radiators were sited in the roof. Jill Bryant as a newcomer in 1943 remembers the classrooms as being cold and her 'awful chilblains itched as the day wore on'. Others appear to have forgotten being cold, yet that must have been the prevailing environment, during the winter. However some do remember that a broken window, not always a result of a pure accident, could create a very cold draught for those sitting nearby. By 1941, as glass became scarce, broken windows, particularly the lower ones were replaced by zinc sheeting and a general air of decay started to set in.

The girls' quadrangle after the war damaged classrooms had been repaired

However some saw this as being done with purposeful intent, to improve the attentiveness of the class. At the front of each classroom was a large fixed blackboard, and at the rear were two cupboards, the venue of a number of pranks to be related later. There seems to have been no provision in the original building for housing the sixth forms.

The school was given additional status by its clock tower, but again, the actual implementation of that was not quite one hundred per cent. The tower had clock faces on each of its four sides, but these rarely showed the same time. Anyone who ventured into the clock room found that each set of hands was driven by a separate and seemingly very under-powered small electric clock motor - four in all. There was a general conviction that in the face of gale-force winds, the hands could individually accelerate or indeed, go backwards. For all that, the clock tower was a very impressive statement.

In the context that it was eventually to find itself, the overall structure of the classrooms provided very little protection in the event of a nearby bomb (which in the high explosive sense, never occurred). Quite early on in the war most of the glass was given a notionally transparent, adhesive film covering. This covering slowly became rather tatty whilst at the same time significantly eroding the transparency of the windows themselves. In about 1943 brick walls were built along the passageway outside the gyms (certainly on the boys'

The Clock Tower

side) and also in proximity to the cloak rooms, presumably to provide some anti blast protection to a central core to which pupils might be ushered in the face of a threat There is some inference that earlier in the war, a sandbag wall had been built on the same line. However, the threat did not arise and the purpose of these walls was never officially explained. I do not recall ever practising assembling there.

The aerial photograph on page 2 shows the school was set in a very large area of playing field, big enough on the boys' side to house two rugby pitches, positioned either side of the cricket square. The girls had hockey pitches and grass and tarmac tennis courts. The drive that separated the girls playing field from the boys is remembered by most pupils of that era as the most potent outward manifestation of the non-fraternisation policy. 'At lunch times we were always being told to stay back a certain number of yards from the drive - I swear that they measured it' recalls Jean Innes. There were undoubtedly exceptions, but on balance it was crossed by either sex during school hours, only on pain of all sorts of sanctions. It was not used by pupils coming to school

and for many years vehicular traffic was confined to a teacher's (Mr W. J. Davies) aged Riley, BGX90.

The two grass quadrangles were essentially identical save that the girls quad had a small greenhouse in it, and the boys quad embraced a simple weather station.

Which really only leaves the cycle sheds. These wooden shelters (again, segregated) were positioned between the school buildings and Broadoak Road and featured in the lives of a great number of the pupils. There was no need to lock up your cycles in those days.

Warts and all it was, nevertheless, a very impressive building for its time.

THE EDUCATION SYSTEM IN THE 1940s.

Weston County School offered a two form entry for both boys and girls, at the age of 11, each form catering for about 30 pupils. The commitment of the parents of anyone joining the school was that their children would stay until at least their 16th birthday, that is, typically for five years. At this point most pupils took the Oxford School Certificate. Pupils then had the option of leaving, or going into the 6th form normally with the aim of taking the (Bristol) Higher School Certificate. For some years this examination regime remained stable and its need and requirements were understood by pupils and teaching staff alike. However from early in the 1950s this structure was dismantled in favour of the General Certificate of Education, of the University of Bristol at Advanced level and at Ordinary level, and then to GCSE's and 'A' levels, regimes that appear to have been in turmoil ever since.

Entry to the School.

The County School was part of the upper tier of state secondary education. If you didn't get a place at the likes of the County School, at least within the state system you went to an 'ordinary' secondary school where up to 1945, schooling normally finished at the age of 14. Alas, that was a significant divide, although by virtue principally of evening class studies, the 'ordinary' route was not necessarily a dead end. Indeed many very professional careers were established on the basis of evening class teaching.

But there was *selection* and for many it was seen as a moment of truth. Marian Hale whose sister was already at the County School, thought 'the alternative of Locking Road Seniors too awful to contemplate and my parents could never have afforded to pay fees'. Whilst waiting for her scholarship results Mary Price, who had, and retains, strong religious convictions prayed that she would get to the County School. But then she wondered what would happen if *everyone* was praying? Her mother assured her 'that God will decide'.

Mary and others made a special effort to prepare for the examination, often encouraged by their school who earmarked likely successful pupils and gave them additional lessons. One of the teachers at Locking Road Junior School, one of the feeder schools to the County School and who were on half day schooling at that time, convened a small group to meet in the nearby Co-op Hall in the afternoon. There were six in the Group, four boys and two girls, and all passed the Scholarship in 1941. This appeared to happen for a number of years, Denis Hodge, Peter Weaver and Jimmy Fisher being beneficiaries, in 1943, for instance.

Selection, in most cases, took the form of that which was generally known as the 'Scholarship' but which officially was the 'examination for the award of special places'. To those who passed, it led to the award of an 'Assisted Place'. This 'Assisted Place' combined an assurance that you were of an adequate academic standard with, subject to parental circumstance, the remission of any fees. Most people entered the County School as a result of that procedure, although there were other ways of entry as we shall see. At least in the short term, they were known as, 'scholarship' boys and girls. The name was an accolade, not a stigma but once established at the school, the different means of entry were not dwelt upon. (Later on, of course, the 'scholarship' became the '11+').

However, there also appeared to be a final endorsement of your suitability, at an interview with the headmistress or headmaster. Jim Owen recalls,

Mr Lindfield sat aloof behind his desk, wearing an academic gown. To an eleven year old, he looked the epitome of a headmaster. His gaze never wavered from my face. One hand holding a fountain pen was poised over a list of names in front of him.

'Tell me how an aeroplane flies'. I burbled something about inclined planes pulling it upwards under the power of its engine. Where the phrase 'inclined planes' had come from, I have no idea. Another man in a Scoutmaster's uniform sat on the edge of a nearby table.

Where is Damascus?' he asked. 'In the Near East' I replied. I had no idea where that was but I had heard it on the radio and thought it

sounded impressive. Mr Lindfield's pen put a dot against one of the names. It looked very much like mine.

'Send in the next boy' he said. And that was that.

However you could pay to go to the County School although this was at the discretion of the head teacher and normally involved a private examination. The number of people so involved was quite small and probably involved special pleading, or perhaps privilege. I entered the evacuated Mitcham County that way, after my father was rather aghast at the near cessation of all schooling after I was evacuated. The fee was four guineas (£4.20) a term, which on an average earnings basis is probably equivalent to about £250 today. Four months later I took the (Somerset) Scholarship, passed, regularised the situation and stopped paying any fees. Janet Lovell (Owen) doesn't remember taking any examination at all but recalls that her mother 'knew Miss Farthing [the Headmistress] quite well'. She joined in mid term and recalls the fee as £4.2.6d (£4.13) a term. Jill Bryant, who had been at the private Stanmore School in Uphill Road North took an entrance exam in 1943, (not 'the scholarship') passed, but her father had to pay a fee of £4-7-6d (£4.38) a term - all around about £250 per term in today's money. Bryan Jones 'failed' the scholarship and his parents eventually paid for him to go to a private school - but he assured them that they were wasting their money. However his brother was already at the County School and when the brother went to the school to bid his farewells prior to joining the armed forces he asked if it

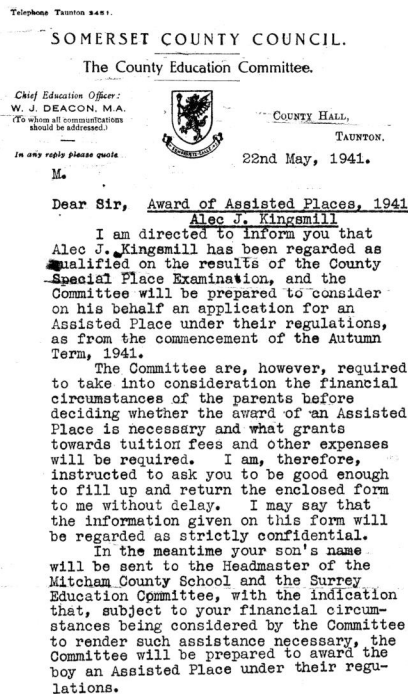

Telephone Taunton 2481.

SOMERSET COUNTY COUNCIL.

The County Education Committee.

Chief Education Officer:
W. J. DEACON, M.A.
(To whom all communications should be addressed)

COUNTY HALL,
TAUNTON.

In any reply please quote

M.

22nd May, 1941.

Dear Sir,   Award of Assisted Places, 1941
            Alec J. Kingsmill
     I am directed to inform you that Alec J. Kingsmill has been regarded as qualified on the results of the County Special Place Examination, and the Committee will be prepared to consider on his behalf an application for an Assisted Place under their regulations, as from the commencement of the Autumn Term, 1941.
     The Committee are, however, required to take into consideration the financial circumstances of the parents before deciding whether the award of an Assisted Place is necessary and what grants towards tuition fees and other expenses will be required. I am, therefore, instructed to ask you to be good enough to fill up and return the enclosed form to me without delay. I may say that the information given on this form will be regarded as strictly confidential.
     In the meantime your son's name will be sent to the Headmaster of the Mitcham County School and the Surrey Education Committee, with the indication that, subject to your financial circumstances being considered by the Committee to render such assistance necessary, the Committee will be prepared to award the boy an Assisted Place under their regulations.

The first indication that you had passed the 'Scholarship'

was yet possible for Bryan to be admitted to the school. Tiny Price (the headmaster) wrote to Bryan's parents almost by return, the result of which was that Bryan took a test at the school and was admitted into the fourth form. Jeff Hynds parents wanted the best for their children and thought that it was most likely obtained at one of the private schools in the town. A doubtful premise to start with, this provision didn't go beyond School Certificate and at that stage Jeff's parents wanted him accepted at the Grammar School. Tiny Price would not agree, saying that Jeff had not passed the 'scholarship'. An appeal to the Somerset Education Committee found only support for Mr Price. So Mr Hynds (Snr.) wrote to Ellen Wilkinson ('Red' Ellen), the fiery Minister of Education in the new post-war Labour Government. She overruled the Somerset authorities and Jeff was admitted to the school. In fact there were those who thought that entrance by means other than overt academic selection (i.e. the Scholarship), improved the 'mix' of the school. As ever, there were ways and means. Yet, the basic entry parameter *was* merit and the process *was* selective. As we shall see, all fees were eventually abolished with the coming of the 1944 Education Act.

The first day could be quite daunting for the newcomers. Jill Bryant remembers sitting cross legged in the hall waiting for her name to be called. She had come from a private school with a class size of 11, and was thus 'overwhelmed' when she found that her new class (1D) had 37 girls in it. The delineators in the girls' school class titles (i.e. the 'D') was normally the first letter of the Form Mistress's surname and no seniority was presumed between the two classes of the same year. The boys did use (a) and (b), or (i) and (ii) with a somewhat uncertain inference of precedence, accompanied by occasional fierce rivalry in the early years.

The Oxford School Certificate

Once at the school, pupils were on a programme of learning aimed fairly single mindedly at eventually passing the Oxford School Certificate in five years time. Of course it wasn't a completely hell bent aim *all* the time, but neither was there a great deal of relief from schooling dominated by classroom based, classic academic subjects. There was 'sport' but even that was virtually compulsory. There wasn't a lot of interaction between pupils and teachers, and at its most basic, you simply learned what was being taught. It was however when one's memory was maybe at its keenest and many have acknowledged the subsequent value in later life of things learned against the odds and without conviction at the time. There were not many 'soft options' available to us, in that era. Nevertheless the syllabus and good facilities also catered for more vocational activities, like art, woodwork and domestic science.

The Oxford School Certificate (other principal universities also administered such Certificates) was introduced in 1858 ' *that the University might convey a great benefit on that large class of persons who cannot afford, or do not require, a University education for their children, by undertaking to examine boys, about their time of their leaving school'.* Other than that girls were added later, that just about sums it up. Most pupils in the 1940s did leave at the end of the fifth form and a 'good' school certificate was an entry, or a starting point, to many careers that had their own training and examination regimes. It was also a route to presumed 'safe' office jobs in local government, banking and insurance, for example. Passing the School Certificate with a sufficient number of subjects and 'credits', meant that you had won 'exemption from London matriculation', which implied in theory that you could go to University, but in practice was taken more as an indication that you had done particularly well, in the School Certificate examination. A minority stayed on, in the sixth form. Of the 39 boys who passed the Oxford School Certificate in 1945 for instance, 10 stayed on to pass the Higher School Certificate two years later, eight eventually seeking a place at University.

Many who left the school at the end of the fifth form saw it in terms of 'getting on with their lives', a decision often endorsed but not always encouraged by their parents. However, sometimes, it *was* the parent's decision.

For the older girls, certainly from 1946, things were more flexible, even imaginative. There, the sixth form included a form called '6th Special' which catered for girls who were not going on to University, but who wished to go on into the sixth whilst waiting, say, for an entry into a profession. Nursing was often a case in point. By its very nature numbers in the class were eroded as the months went by, from nine down to two in 1946/1947, for instance. Besides a broad range of academic subjects, shorthand and bookkeeping were also included in the syllabus, in this class.

The Higher School Certificate and Scholarships

By the time one started studying for the Higher School Certificate, typically at 16, one's future career was taking on a certain fixed direction. The career path was almost entirely dependant on a gut feeling in the almost total absence of any career guidance. This lack of any career guidance, even in respect of an eventual application to a University, is probably the most fundamental criticism of the school, that has surfaced in recent contacts with my contemporaries. Pupils normally took three subjects in Higher and these covered a fairly narrow field. Certainly the Arts and Science divide was by then pretty immutable, a circumstance that Denis Hodge realised later in life when his vocation migrated from medicine, to the Church. Universities at that time were still fee based and this cost could only be avoided (or at least, paid for by others) by choosing teaching as a career, in which case the Department of Education paid, or by winning a scholarship. Otherwise it was down to your parents. These scholarships, awarded by the University themselves, by the State or by the Local Education Authority (LEA) were hard to come by. The University ones were normally awarded on the basis of special examinations; the State and the LEA ones normally as a result of the Higher School Certificate results. The local scholarships were the most numerous but up to 1947 there were only 8 of those for the whole of Somerset, increased to 20, in 1948. Thus when pupils from the Boys school won five County Scholarships in 1949, they had secured 25% of those on offer for boys and girls alike, in the whole of Somerset. For the majority, most University Scholarship examinations were entered more as a trial run for Higher, than that there would be any chance of winning one. Going on to University remained a minority pastime.

The Weston schools took a more defined role in the state education scheme, when as a result of the provisions of the 1944 Education Act they became the 'Weston-super-Mare Grammar School for Boys' and the 'Weston-super-Mare Grammar School for Girls', in 1945. This reflected the proposals for post war education brought in by 'Rab' Butler, the Minister for Education in the wartime coalition Government, and enacted by them. This provided full time education now up to a minimum age of 15, within regimes established by local education authorities, although the regimes themselves had to be within a framework stipulated by the Ministry of Education. The framework for secondary education was bounded by three types of school - Grammar, Secondary Modern and Technical. The intention was that there would be no selection on the basis of a competitive exam. Instead people would be initially allocated into one or other stream on the basis of an 'assessment of individual aptitudes' and 'a regard for parents' wishes'. All streams would be seen to be equal in status and there was to be ready provision for people to move seamlessly between the streams, as an individual's interests or talents developed. All school fees were abolished.

Like so much of post war education theory, although full of good intent this was in fact pious nonsense. Even by 1946, the boys school was receiving 170 applications for the 66 places available. The tripartite division into Grammar, Technical and Modern, equitable and reasonable though it at first seemed, proved to be much more rigid in practice than its originators had hoped. Thus the scholarship, now the 11+, had to be retained. This was anathema to the political fraternity and to much education thinking at that time, indeed until this day, and solace was

eventually found in Somerset, in 'comprehensive' education. Thus the Weston Grammar Schools were closed in 1971, and merged organisationally with Uphill Secondary Modern School, to become 'Broadoak Comprehensive'. Since then the organisation of educational provision in Britain has experienced over 40 years of controversy, constant change, confusion and chaos. Some saw the final winding back of the wall that divided the main hall into two, as the final symbolic act of the old regime, and welcoming in a new beginning. Others saw the destruction of the Grammar Schools as an act of educational vandalism. The comprehensive name lasted until 1999 when the decaying school buildings were demolished and a new 'Broadoak Community School' was built and established on part of the onetime playing fields. The school, despite the name change, remains as an all-ability comprehensive. An attempt by the authorities to earmark the space vacated by the old school buildings for housing, was vigorously opposed and it is now retained as an open space.

Miss G. E. Farthing

However all that was beyond our decade.

THE HEADMISTRESS AND THE HEADMASTERS.

Miss G. E. Farthing BA was the girls' headmistress from the establishment of the school in 1935 and for the whole of the 1940's. For the boys, **Mr. T. E. Lindfield MA**, who started the original school at Nithsdale Road in 1922 and was the Head there, became the first Head of the Boys' school at Broadoak Road and remained so until December 1942. He was followed by **Mr F. R. Price MA (Cantab.)** as the boys' Head for the rest of the decade.

All were rather aloof characters although perhaps, not untypical for their time. The boys' headmasters never seemed really at ease with their pupils (perhaps they were not meant to be) and the core relationship seemed to be based mainly on the imposition of standards and of discipline. I don't think that I had even the most cursory conversation with Mr.Price during the six years that our years at the school overlapped. And yet this lady and these gentlemen imposed regimes on the schools which stood them, and in retrospect their pupils, in good stead through very difficult times. It was the era of the stiff upper lip which they very much exemplified, and not the era of counselling or of fortunes spent at the florists.

Miss Farthing did in fact have a nickname, it was 'Jane' - no one seems to know why - although her Christian name was Gertrude. She was a graduate from London University with a degree in modern languages and her association with the school also went back to the Nithsdale Road days, where she was the Senior Mistress. At the County school, particularly during the war years, she taught French, scripture and arithmetic, although someone has written that they were so scared of her that they didn't learn a thing. One pupil recalls that somehow Miss Farthing often managed to orientate the lesson after about ten minutes into stories about her cats. She was a chain smoker and sometimes required a pupil to buy cigarettes for her, from a shop in Moorland Road. However there does not appear to

Mr T. E. Lindfield

have been a single element of school life that did not reflect some aspect of her authority, and in no area was this stronger than in the behaviour and the moral protection of her girls. She really did appear to fear the outcome of any association with boys - perhaps no more than a fear that such contact would distract them from their studies. As we shall mention again later, Miss Farthing was wholly opposed to girls participating in athletics. To be called into the presence of Miss Farthing for some discipline misdemeanour put fear and dread into the most hardy. Her simple command 'Come', to those waiting outside her study, 'turned legs to jelly'. Yet there are also many records of pupils

acknowledging the respect and affection that they felt for her. Miss Farthing eventually retired in 1956, having been at the school for 34 years.

Mr T.E. Lindfield had the nickname 'slink' seemingly reflecting his habit of creeping around the school premises in search of a misdemeanour. He had a long history with the school as headmaster but few seem to have recalled anything approaching any casual dealing with him. He never wrote any notes in the school magazine save at the outbreak of war and on his departure, but those did infer some compassion with the world as it was. He also had an uncompromising attitude towards any excursion from the standards that he expected, particularly in terms of behaviour whilst in school uniform. To be even seen in a fish and chip shop in school uniform was a serious misdemeanour. To reflect his unfamiliarity with the whole concept, he called the meal 'chips and fish'. Mr Lindfield, alas, left the school, under a cloud. He was accused of claiming pay for fire watch duties, whilst still at home. A special sub committee of the Somerset Education committee did not accept his solicitors view that Mr Lindfield was within the terms of his assignment by being available at his nearby home, to

Mr F.R. Price

which he had a direct telephone line. On a less legalistic defence, others thought that he was simply ill-equipped to spend the night time hours in the close company of members of his staff, or even, worse, with school prefects. During the war, others of course, had made bigger sacrifices. His punishment was serious. He was then 60 and eligible for retirement but in the wartime circumstance he would have expected to have been offered continuing employment. In fact the committee made the decision that this should not happen. There were many rumours about this event but that was how it was eventually told, in fact headlined, in the 'Weston Gazette' - a local newspaper of the time. Contrary to many rumours, the dates which featured in the indictment did not include the night when the girls' school was burned down. No parents were invited to his final Speech Day. It was a very sad end.

This bought Mr F.R. Price to our domain. There is an inference that Mr W.J.Davies, a senior master and a school stalwart, coveted this role and for this reason his relationship with Mr.Price was never entirely cordial. Because of Mr.Price's height (around 6'3") he was known to everyone as 'Tiny'. He is the only one of the three, for whom I could find any sort of biography. The first thing that I learned was that his Christian names were Francis Rowland - I never knew that. He was born at Westcliff, Essex, was at Cambridge, completing tripos in English and French in 1927. He was a senior master in both those subjects at Watford Grammar School until 1942, when he came to Weston as headmaster of the Boys' School. He left in 1951. He would have been 36 years old when he came to Weston, a young man by most standards but he remained very aloof. His only outward role was primarily in the imposition of standards, although he did occasionally take scripture, and a sort of Civics. I can never remember him showing the slightest interest in the Scouts for instance, even by way of a casual visit, although we were a school troop. He did appear occasionally on the touch line at a school rugby match. One insight into Mr Price comes from Gerald Martin. After the 1946 'mock Oxford', and just prior to the School Certificate examinations, Mr Price called on Gerald's father - they all lived near the school. Mr Price told Mr. Martin (Snr.) that the staff had no confidence in his son's ability to pass the exam and therefore the school would not pay his entry fee. If his father would pay the fee, which he agreed to do, he would be entered with the rest. In fact Gerald passed quite well, but his father never asked about this error of judgement on the part of the school. There was no such problem when Gerald took Higher. Paul Warren has a tale somewhat in the same vein. Whilst in the lower sixth, Paul's father died suddenly. Mr Price called Paul to his office. Price told him that as his father's pension had died with him, his mother would have no money to support him at university and the grants available would not be sufficient and therefore he should give up any thoughts of going to University, and think instead of a career in the Civil Service. It might well have represented the pragmatic view, but Mr Price certainly seemed an emissary for the world of hard knocks.

In 1951, Mr Price went on to the much larger Southend High School for Boys. Their centenary book acknowledges that F.R.Price 'brought a moral earnestness that left its mark. Even if his standards and expectations took some living up to, the school was a better place because of them He left the School as a grammar school as it had been on his arrival [and still is].

He had been determined to keep it a grammar school against, as he would have said, outside trends' One wonders what Mr. Price might have done for the Weston Grammar Schools, had he stayed.

Elsewhere in this narrative there are other individual recollections of these three august entities. Overall, I suppose that they just ran a very tight ship, appropriate for the age. They taught a resilience that many have acknowledged to have stood them in good stead, in later life.

THE BOYS' SCHOOL STAFF

For this chapter I am very much indebted to Derek Porter who in his own personal memoirs, "Write it down, Dad. A response" has written extensively and amusingly about the teachers that taught him at the County School. Many others have written individual anecdotes about their teachers, and the School Magazine has bought a measure of additional detail to the recollection of the teachers of our era. This chapter attempts to combine them all - yet with a heavy indebtedness to Derek, whose words are italicised in what follows.

Who, I wonder, of the Autumn term of 1940 can fail to remember Mr F.R. Bateman? We called him 'Freddie', but he was also known as 'Fungus', in acknowledgement of his large, unruly, moustache. He was about to retire from another school in Weston - or, perhaps, had retired - when he took a position at the County School to fill one of the several gaps that had been caused by the call-up of some of the younger staff. To a boy of eleven any one over, say, thirty seems ancient so actual age was of no interest or consequence. What was of interest, and concern to some, was his method of keeping discipline. He had a commanding presence and brooked no nonsense and this was made manifest by his manner of awarding detentions for misbehaving - mostly inattention. 'Boy !' he would shout, 'What's your name?!' On being told, he would whip out a little black book from the inside pocket of his jacket and bellow ' Your name goes down once!' Three entries and the final result was a Saturday morning detention. I also remember him as a good teacher of basics who really drummed information and learning into his pupils. His main subject was mathematics but I see from my report book that during my first three years he took my class for English, History, and even Art!"

As is recorded in another chapter, Mr. Bateman rescinded all detentions, on hearing of the sinking of the 'Bismarck'. He left the school during the Summer Term of 1945, due to ill health, having come virtually out of retirement to serve the war years.

French was mostly taught to Derek's form by **Mr H. C. Wood.**

H. C. Wood - wished to be called Monsieur Dubois, but was of course called 'Woody' behind his back or, later on, 'Skip', when he was our respected Scout Master. He was firm but friendly, a good teacher who brought out the best in an individual. I enjoyed being in his charge, especially in the Scouts and would have been mortified to offend him. He was clearly a big influence in my school life and I was naturally sorry when he left after I had been in the sixth form for one term".

H. C. Wood who had joined the school in January 1936, left the County School at the end of 1944, to take up a post at Burton High School, in Derbyshire. His successor for a short while as French teacher was the headmaster - Mr. F.R.Price. Mr L. A. Webb then came for a short while and then Mr E. S. Rue came for a more prolonged stay.

Mr F. J. Hill *was not only our History Master but also our Assistant Scout Master. As the ASM he was a very good foil to Skip because he, being tall and, to us, somewhat austere, gave a good balance to the Troop leadership. It was a story known to all, even though it may well have been apocryphal, that he obtained his nickname when he would call Scouts for second helpings of food when at camp. The cry of 'anyone for more fud?' made it inevitable that thenceforth he was always known as 'Fud' Hill. History particularly in the fifth form was a very defined area for study, from 1830 until the not very modern. For Mr Hill, presentation was the name of the game. Mr. Hill insisted that in any written response, main headings had to be in capital letters and underlined twice; sub headings underlined once. Sections were written in capital letters; subsections indented in lower case. Numerals and letters had their assigned places in the layout of the text".*

It was pedantic in the extreme but Derek admits that the general principles served him in good stead when writing reports during his career. "It was almost unbelievable but twenty-four years later my eldest son Christopher", continues Derek, "had *exactly* the same lesson as *his* first lesson in History" Father and son both progressed to the same lessons about Worlebury and its stone-age encampment --- history written on tablets of stone.

Nevertheless in later years Mr. Hill managed to get Derek, and many of his co-pupils, to commit to memory sufficient events and dates to enable them to get through the School Certificate exam. Mr. Hill had a complete conviction about the worth of remembering certain well known utterances of the big players of those times. Nearly sixty years later I can readily recall 'I have called the New World into existence to redress the balance of the old' (Canning recognising the one-time south American Spanish colonies in 1826); 'We must educate our masters' (an observation by Viscount Sherbrooke, in 1857 commenting on the recently passed Reform Act (in fact this was a popularised version of a rather more pedantic observation) and 'My mission is to pacify Ireland' (a somewhat over optimistic observation of Gladstone's in 1868). I am sure that I could dredge up quite a few more. My own school certificate results were pretty modest and I only got one 'Very Good' and that was in History. I am wholly indebted to 'Fud' Hill for that result.

Latin - not exactly my favourite subject but one that was enlivened by the character of the master whose name was **Mr. H. H. Lawrence** *but who was universally known as Mike. I can see and hear him now, opening the classroom door and striding rapidly across to his desk saying, in a very loud voice ' Discipuli, pictorum, spectate ! By the time that he had reached his desk he had added a page number, and the lesson was in full swing. The lesson continued in this fashion until its end. He wobbled to and from school on a very rusty bicycle that even then looked as if it was about to fall to pieces at any moment. Once again Derek's son remembers the same master and, in this case, the same bike: indeed, it was by then so bad that the police ignored it in the cycle shed, during an inspection, on the grounds that it could not possibly be in use!". Others recall Mr Lawrence exclaiming 'there's an itch in my hand' when behaviour was faltering.*

Mathematics was given a new twist in the fourth form when **Mr C. W. Pinton** *was given the unenviable task of trying to install some knowledge into my class. Whereas Mr. Bateman had been rather loud and something of a strict disciplinarian, 'Charlie' was usually quiet and gentle. Slowly, but very thoroughly, he led us further into the intricacies of algebra and through the puzzles of Euclid at the rate of one theorem per lesson. Outside the classroom he was a great lover of cricket and it did not need very much to divert him from our proper course of study. On one memorable occasion he needed no hint that cricket was a much more interesting subject than Geometry for, turning from the blackboard on which he had been writing, he asked ' What's a no-ball, Porter?' The laws of the game made a very acceptable topic for the rest of the lesson!*

Unfortunately Mr. Pinton was away ill for a period whilst Derek was in the fifth form and he was substituted by a recent newcomer to the school, **Mr C. N. Harris**. Later, in the sixth form, many of us had every reason to be grateful to Mr. Harris for he was an excellent teacher and gave us a good feel for both Pure and Applied Mathematics. However, on his first appearance before us, and this was separately in both form 5(a) and form 5(b), both forms were knocked sideways by the fact that on each occasion he swept into the classroom, drew five circles that covered the blackboard, and set about the proofs of five theorems more or less, as one. This was productivity of an entirely new order and it was a surprise to no-one that thereafter he was always known as 'Speedy' - 'Speedy' Harris. Some recall Mr Harris as a lay preacher at the Gospel Hall, in Waterloo Street.

My list is not yet complete for there are others who could not help but remain memorable! **Mr W. J. Davies** *is one such. 'Bill' - or 'Old Bill' - as he was always called (but not to his face) was the Physics master and also the form-master for the sixth form. The syllabus was obviously far too wide, or he thought that we were too thick to take it all in, because the whole topic of Electricity and Magnetism was omitted. Amends were made in the sixth form when he had no alternative but to teach it. He had the very disconcerting habit of emphasizing a point that he was making - particularly when he believed that some wrong had been done, or some vital point missed, by punching one on the arm. In no way was this done to hurt because they were not delivered with force, but the several pummels that one received to reinforce his point left one in no doubt that punishment had been administered.* Bill was a trialist for the Welsh rugby team - perhaps he even played? - and he certainly took a very close interest in the School's endeavours, and in individual players. Denis Hodge, a later general practitioner, remembers Bill having 'a recognisable rugby injury gait' and 'he allowed the laboratory door to be left ajar to teach us that the angle of incidence always equals the angle of reflection'. On a somewhat different note, who could forget BGX 90, Bill Davies' old fabric-roof-covered Riley? To the best of our recollection he was the only member of staff to drive majestically up the drive, to the school buildings.

Another stalwart of the staff was **Mr A. R. Robinson***, the woodwork master, otherwise known as 'Robbie' or 'Snug'. His mission in life was to try to get the uninterested, incompetent, lazy students to make such advanced things as a mortise and tenon joint, or, holy of holiest, a joint with dovetails! The blackboard rubber, or a suitable piece of wood, often hurtled across the workshop to startle the unwary. My prowess with a piece of wood, a plane, a chisel, and a mallet was pitiful and left me marvelling at Robbie's own skill which was legendary. In no time at all he would 'knock-up' a specimen of whatever it was that we were labouring at that day. Later, in the fifth and sixth forms, I was able to switch to Engineering Drawing, a subject which I found much more to my liking and better suited to my abilities. It was during this time that I really came to appreciate his skill with chalk on the blackboard. He could make the most intricate engineering drawings on the blackboard with the aid of only a T-square and a set-square, and at the same time address the class and keep his eye on whatever might be going on".*

In Derek's third year in the sixth-form he was granted permission to allocate five periods to drawing and, through Robbie's interest and guidance, he learnt much that later stood him in good stead. Mr. Robinson had in fact been away from the school for four years till Autumn 1944, first as an instructor, then in charge of Technical Lectures at a Government Training Centre.

Another inhabitant of the staff-room was **Mr A. B. Davis** *- 'Archie' by popular acclaim. He taught English and was committed to ensuring that as many as possible passed the School Certificate exam. He must have known that he was facing a losing battle as far as English Literature was concerned because he resorted to cramming in an unusual way. The plot of the play or the set book was important in that it set the general scene, but inevitably not everything could be remembered. Shakespeare would, I imagine, have been horrified to know that his 'The Merchant of Venice' was divided into passages labelled 'A' 'B' or 'C'! Over many years, Archie had observed that examiners asked questions about certain scenes in the set play and had accordingly devised his system of helping us beat them. Those passages awarded an 'A' had to be learnt by heart; those accorded a 'B' could be learnt perhaps just a little less well; whilst those only deserving of a 'C' should at the very least be understood It was one thing to pass an exam but quite another to acquire an appreciation of Shakespeare. The set book in 1945 was 'Travels with a Donkey in the Cevennes' by Robert Louis Stevenson but, for similar reasons to the above, Derek remembers little about it save for the one thing which led to a well used catchword during the rest of his time at school. When Stevenson's donkey had a fit of the sulks and refused to budge, the weary traveller resorted to jabbing it with a pin tied to the end of a stick. Nothing very peculiar about that, you might say, and you would be right - but it was the magic word 'proot!' which was alleged to work the miracle and get the animal moving. Thenceforth, in real life, 'proot' became a greeting, a farewell, a term of fellowship, or anything else that the speaker meant to convey and strangely enough, the hearer could always interpret it correctly! It may be called boyish humour but a strange bond developed between the 'prooters.* I share all these recollections of Derek's although I additionally remember a Stevenson viewpoint in 'Travels with a Donkey' that ' it was better to travel than to arrive'. For many years I thought that a good philosophy and in some measure acted upon it. Mr A.B.Davies retired in 1953, having been at the school for 25 years.

Mr Thomas, although a boys' school teacher, taught music to both the girls school and the boys. Such were the limitations of those times, 'music' in class was almost confined to singing, whilst other musical activities were centred on the Music Society and the embryonic school orchestra. Very Welsh in temperament, Mr Thomas - Tommy - helped school rugby to survive through the war. Mr Thomas held sway mainly in the Moorland Road church hall and those who were musically blessed, held Mr. Thomas in some esteem. Others remember the lessons more for the time that could be wasted getting to Moorland Road and back, and for a while, the lardy cakes that could be bought at the bakers in Moorland Road. But Mr Thomas was a fine pianist, and a gifted musician. He had a notable talent for training choirs; the school choir excelled on many public occasions and he also formed a male voice choir - the Lyrian Singers - which gave public concerts at the Winter Gardens and the Rozel Bandstand.

Two masters joined HM Forces quite early on in the war - Mr. White who initially joined the Royal Artillery, and Mr. Walters who joined the Royal Air Force. Promoted to Major, Mr. White migrated to the Royal Army Ordnance Corps stationed in India. Flight Lieutenant Walters worked in communications and later transferred to the Education Branch of the R.A.F. Both returned to the school during the summer of 1946.

Mr G. A. White, otherwise known as George or 'Joey', was much liked. He taught Geography, but his main prowess was on the sports field or in the gym. He was a fine athlete himself and had played a number of times for the Somerset Rugby XV, and was also selected as a reserve for the England side in 1940. It was widely rumoured that in fact he had been a major in the Commandos and had fought in the jungle. This, it was believed, was why he built formidable assault courses in the gym, and made his charges go over them like soldiers. Despite this prowess, Denis Hodge recalls that Mr. White was very encouraging 'to the less talented, a fact which has remained an object lesson for me'. Not only did the boys like him, but so did the girls. Perhaps using modern terminology, one lady informant describes him as 'dishy' and others confess to coming to watch their boy friends play rugger, 'if Mr. White was refereeing'. However he seemed short of quirks, and hardly any anecdotes about him have surfaced. He was widely respected both in and outside the school. He was president of the local branch of the Burma Star Association. He took a keen interest in local government, and was at one time, Mayor of Weston. Mr White died in February 2003, having attended one of the school reunions not that long before.

Mr R. A. Walters ('Windy Walters' to all) taught biology. Denis Hodge remembers him with affection. Denis remembers Mr. Walters for his interest in tropical fish and for his outings to the Mendips for 'ecology' and for the diversion Mr. Walters enjoyed at the local hostelry, whilst his pupils were left 'to identify every plant in a square yard' Denis remembers Mr. Walter's car's number plate - BUP693 -

which Mr Walters said stood for 'buggered up for petrol', when petrol was scarce. Prior to his call up he gave the occasional lift to school in his car to June Hale, who lived almost opposite him. Mr Walters also helped with the school's Air Training Corps unit. He had had considerable experience of training wireless operators during his five years in the R.A.F.

Those were the teachers that Derek most remembers but there were others...

Mr (later Rev.) J. G. Holmes BA,B.Sc,BD joined the School in 1926 as Senior mathematics master and remained for 17 years. Inevitably, he was known as 'Sherlock'. He had been a keen rugby player in his early days and had played as a forward for Devon, but a serious arm wound sustained in the First World War when he was an officer in the Devonshire Regiment, put paid to those endeavours. He took holy orders in 1940, and in 1943 he decided to give up teaching and he joined the Royal Naval Volunteer Reserve, as a Chaplain, but he died in April 1945 after a short illness. He seems to have been remembered with genuine affection by both staff and pupils, the latter occasionally trying to divert his lesson to his views on life in general, which were cherished by everyone . This could be successful - but not always.

The appointment of **Miss Dorothy Miller** ('Dusty' Miller), in 1943, was an innovation. She was the first lady to be offered a permanent appointment at the boys' school. She taught Geography and also participated in work in the gym. She also gave valuable assistance at the Harvest Camps. My own recollection was of the sheer quality of the free hand maps she drew with coloured chalks on the blackboard and indeed, of her teaching overall. Otherwise my recollections err towards the totally immature and just occasionally unpleasant way she was treated by just a few of our fellows. I do hope that she had happier memories than that. I am sure that we saw in this boorish behaviour the downside of the school's vigorous segregation of boys and girls. However there was an upside. One respondent recalls thinking she was 'quite beautiful', yet recalls his embarrassment at having to hold her legs when she was teaching his class how to do handstands. He dropped her! Another lad has said 'who could forget Dusty Miller? - his reminder came in the form of her entry in his autograph book 'A thing of beauty is a joy for ever'. He was pleased to concur. Miss Miller left at the end of the Summer Term in 1946. Like so many of our teachers, no one of us really knew the true person behind the public face.

Mr J. R. Hay, known to all as 'Curly', because of the paucity of any golden locks, taught Chemistry. Except for at the very outset of its inception, he was also in charge of the Air Training Corps Squadron, based at the school. He was a man of a certain worn appearance, almost gaunt, never seemingly in the best of health, but everyone said that that was due to him having only one lung after being gassed in the first World War. Indeed it was so - he was a victim of Phosgene poisoning. To those for whom Chemistry was a chore, 'Curley' Hay probably seemed to err towards the severe and the humourless. To those for whom the subject had interest or was of particular relevance, Mr Hay was seen as a teacher with a brilliant mind. Three pupils in particular who eventually followed a career in medicine felt his influence as being substantial. One of them has subsequently observed that ' it was very poignant to visit him in retirement in reduced circumstances, very poor health and blindness. It was so unjustified. Why didn't we do more for him?'.

Other masters simply did a good job in a fashion that hasn't left a great aftermath of recollection. **Mr R. H. Pope** ('Reggie') was one such. He taught French - normally you had either H.C. Wood or you had Mr. Pope. I had Mr Pope throughout my stay. Although the teaching approach was what I think you might describe as rigid and academic and a bit short of humour, I remain surprised at how much I remember of my French. It has stood me in good stead a number of times, if only in Turkey in the 'fifties where it was still the second language. Since then I have confronted, and against all odds tried to learn (even needed to learn) a number of other languages, including a rather expensive Berlitz 'total immersion' course in Swedish, but in none of them could I now count up to ten. However, my French stays surprisingly useful. I am very much indebted to Mr. Pope. One quirk of the eventual school certificate exam in French was that if you passed French 'Oral', you were deemed to have passed the Interpreter badge of the Scouts. This not only permitted you to disport the appropriate badge on your sleeve but also to sew on, an embroidered 'Parle Francais' above your right breast pocket. I remember well that it was the first thing that we removed before going to the Jamboree, near Paris, in 1947. It was a claim that we were *very* reluctant to make in the presence of the locals.

Mr E. T. Bucknall joined the school in 1941, almost in retirement, from the private sector to teach Chemistry and General Science. He had a pronounced Somerset accent, knew his subject backwards and had apparently written five books about it. He had an infantry officer son, Dick Bucknell, of whom he was justifiably proud.

Mr Donald Mather M.A.(Cantab.) came in 1946 to teach English and stayed for eight years. He taught a range of classes including the 6th Science group, fearful perhaps that they would forget the basics of grammar and composition. I remember one epithet written by Mr Mather

on my end of term report was, 'Shows a clarity of thought, occasionally marred by faults in style'. No doubt, it still shows. Mr Mather was probably the first of the post war new school of teachers, with a much more relaxed teacher-pupil relationship. Others were, of course, to follow. But it is sobering to realise our new teacher of those days is now 88 (2005). He lives in Surrey and recently wrote to say 'I started my professional career in Weston-super-Mare Grammar School and never looked back, so I have fond memories of the school, the town and its amateur dramatic societies'.

THE GIRLS' SCHOOL STAFF

There are many recollections , both affectionate and just occasionally uncertain, from the past pupils of the girls' school.

First we seem to have **Miss R. L. Berlandina**, believed to have been Swedish and who took gym, in the early years of the decade. June Hale remembers her mainly for her insistence that girls should have a shower after any gym lesson. Any attempt to settle for a quick immersion of the feet only, was roundly condemned. Since gym lessons often had to be fitted in, in the length of an ordinary classroom period, getting dry in time could be a miserable process. Miss Berlandina 'had a delightfully broken English accent', but left the school about 1943.

Then in the same vocation, indeed her replacement, was **Miss Nora R Bennet**, who took gym and games and 'always wore turquoise lyle stockings, hooded cloak and gloves, when we played hockey' remembers Valerie Champion 'We froze, she didn't'. Valerie additionally recalls that Miss Bennet had no sympathy with her when she complained of earache, and Judy Price recalls 'that she almost drowned me at Knightstone baths by making me jump into the water over my head, at the count of ten'. Marian Hale has eschewed any attempt at diving after Miss Bennett pushed her in head first in an attempt to encourage her. Miss Bennet, it would seem, was the archetypal games mistress, with firm favourites among those who were good at PE, but was unsympathetic to those who weren't. But there is no doubt that under Miss Bennet the school teams - hockey, netball and tennis - did remarkably well, and former players remember her 'excellent tuition', and the sense of camaraderie she engendered. Miss Bennett always wore a divided skirt and springy shoes except on Speech Day 'when she was transformed'.

Miss A. M. Boome seems to have been known variously as 'Annabella', 'Arabella Maud' or 'Katy'. She took French. She 'resembled 'Olive Oil' of Popeye fame but always wore beautiful tweeds and knitted stockings' observes one contributor. Someone else has volunteered that 'Miss Boome had the unfortunate habit of spitting over you if you happened to be in the front row when she was enunciating her verbs' although it appears to have all be worthwhile for the informant affirms that she still retains enough French 'to use at appropriate moments'. Another observer has commented that she was quite tall, aristocratic looking, and wore her hair in a bun. She was seen as a very superior 'county' lady. She talked of her ancestors and had a family crest. She asked her pupils if their families had such crests. Bernice Brookman feels that Miss Boome wasn't entirely at ease with her Weston Grammar School pupils for she let it be known that in her previous post she had been used to teaching 'young ladies'. In 1952, she was seriously ill with cancer in Bristol General Hospital.

Mrs E. R. Bourke - a 'little old lady' taught scripture and French. Mary Price has said that she was helped 'by this most enthusiastic R.E. teacher'. She produced wonderful little blackboard drawings - a very kindly lady, liked by everyone.

Miss Sylvia R. Brice taught English. Her nickname was 'Fanny B'. One of the school stalwarts she appears to have generated a wide spectrum of recollections. Mary Price has written that she is eternally grateful to Miss Brice 'for insisting that we wrote and spoke grammatically - I can still hear her voice'. Jean Cooke says that because of Miss Brice, her enthusiasm for English literature has stayed with her to the present time, especially for poetry. Miss Brice also taught History of Art, about which she was very knowledgeable. Not everyone appreciated her - at least one ex-pupil remembers her as 'sour with no sense of humour' Her dress sense was very much her own, convinced that fashion repeated itself over 10 year cycles. She believed that if you kept your clothes long enough they would again become fashionable. Another recollection was that she had a lisp and spoke with an 'Oxford drawl'. Roy Perry who was in one of the mixed sixth form classes, thought that she was 'excellent'.

However someone has complained that Miss Bryce 'wouldn't let me sing in school concert', and someone else has said that she was 'very sarcastic. She wiped the floor with us if we answered her questions incorrectly - so I was always afraid to put up my hand'. For Judy Price 'perhaps the greatest influence came from Miss Brice. Her knowledge of English Literature and her ability to instil it into her pupils was exemplary'. Alison Day's observations seem to imply quite a heavy work load with Miss Bryce, with at least three classical books a term, two plays, plus poetry and grammar. Miss Brice lived in Clevedon and travelled to school each day in a car shared with her friend Miss Shepherd. However, occasionally she would

do a bit of police duty on the Clevedon train, to ensure that the segregation policy was working. She produced several books of poetry after she retired, and Joy Pinton who continued to visit her until she died, remembers that she, among others, was 'encouraged' to buy them, with the proceeds going to good causes.

For **Miss Campbell**, we have only the words of Frank Ashby. His link with her and his knight-like attempt to save her books and belongings at the height of the school fire during the June 1942 air raid are given later, in his account of that event. She left in 1943.

Miss Marion R. Caws, seemingly of a younger background also taught French, and appeared to have a nudge-nudge, wink wink, sympathy for the Free French forces. Some girls seem to recall that she sold badges to them, in support of the Free French. She was an enthusiastic teacher, if rather eccentric, and could create interest in even the most arcane of French writers, or so they seemed at the time, like the seventeenth century fables of La Fontaine. She must also have had an interest in the Pythagorean doctrine of transmigration of souls, for she believed, apparently, that she was descended from Queen Nefertiti's cat. However she also seems to have had a ferocious temper to go with this feline image, and 'if she lost it (her temper), it was the end of the lesson'. She had a long illness in 1943 and pupils including Ann Bray, used to visit her at home taking on one occasion, 'enough bluebells to stock Weston Woods'.

Miss Crystal taught history, and perhaps Maths to the first form. She was 'like a breath of Spring....we could talk to her'. 'We worried about Miss Crystal's heart condition and thought it very romantic when she married' confides a past pupil. She became Mrs. Turner in 1942 and left the school in 1944. She told Valerie Champion's mother that Valerie was 'accurate but untidy'.

Miss J. Denton, known as 'Dizzy' taught History. She began at the school in 1946, but subsequently had a breakdown.

Miss Olive Frampton also taught English. To one past pupil, she 'seemed human; her academic gown billowed as she sailed along the corridors; she always had the scent of perfume around her, *eau de cologne* I think; an inspiring and encouraging teacher'. Though with somewhat different recollection of the perfume in question, this is echoed by Jill Bryant who remembers Miss Frampton wafting *lavender* perfume. Jean Innes recalls that 'I was 12 years old when I read out one of my essays in the class and Miss Frampton said that I was going to be a writer'. Jean has indeed become a very successful novelist. Alas someone recalls that '(I) got three order marks in my first week earning Miss Frampton's disapproval for my entire time at the school'. Marian

Hale acknowledges that 'I am especially grateful to Miss Frampton for giving me a good grounding in English grammar and a love of Shakespeare, and indirectly, drama'.

Miss Margaret M. Greenwood taught Maths and Scripture. She seemed very young to pupils in 1944 and Jean Ashley appreciated her as her first Form Mistress. But at least one other ex-pupil remembers her as 'nasty'. However, 'Fud' Hill the boys history master, a widower and quite a bit older than her, evidently didn't agree, for they were eventually married.

Miss Harding, seemingly in later years, taught music. Judy Price recalls that 'by personality and a sense of joy in her subject [she] introduced me to the delights of classical music'

Miss Beryl Hughes took Latin. Roy Perry recalls the time when he and Sheila Strange were the only two sixth formers taking Higher School Latin with Miss Hughes. He enjoyed the arrangement which he thought was 'very cosy', and regarded her as a very fine teacher. She was herself a pupil at the school in the Nithsdale Road era, from 1926 to 1933, eventually returning as a teacher from 1944 to 1980, though, she says, for the last year or so of her 36 years teaching at the school she was 'only filling in, when called'. Miss Hughes still lives in Weston and although not able to come to reunions she appreciates hearing about the activities of Old Westonians and sends her good wishes to everyone. At the time of writing (2005) she will be nearing 90. Like many teachers of yesteryear, Miss Hughes could be strict and uncompromising. One former pupil, still smarting somewhat from the perceived injustice of it, recalls an incident when Miss Hughes 'was so incensed that she had to send me out of a Latin lesson, that she blocked my inclusion in a group that was to go to watch tennis at Wimbledon'. *Nemo me impune lacessit* (as Miss Hughes might have said.) Her sister, **Miss Majorie Hughes** taught Maths. They were both very involved with the Girl Guide movement and were collectively known as 'the Stuggetts' (!?)

Mr R. Kinghorn taught Physics and Chemistry, and 'looked like Danny Kaye'. He had ginger hair and a matching complexion. Because of the bomb damage, Mr Kinghorn would take the girls in the boys' science laboratories, which overlooked the rugby pitches, 'which the girls appreciated'.

Miss E. Lyons taught Chemistry. Her nickname was 'Leo'. She hailed from Northern Ireland and joined the staff in 1941. She was thought to be 'a very nice lady with a lovely accent'. Ann Bray and Barbara Morrill would have heard less of it than some, since they took turns regularly to be sent out of the classroom for talking in her lessons.

At Easter 1945, she married Maurice Bickley, who was in the Royal Navy, and also the son of the Minister of Boulevard Congregational Church. She left the school in the summer of that year.

Miss Marie Measures also took Latin - a lovely lady - got married.

Miss Moss and Miss White

Not a great deal more than that has come to light, except a little story from a former pupil, who wishes only to be known as Mary, since she has always been rather shy. At school Mary had a high regard for Miss Measures, but she surprised even herself when, on the day she was leaving and was excited about it, she found herself forgetting her shyness and blurting out to Miss Measures, 'I'll buy you an ice cream with my first wage packet!' Amazed at her unheard of temerity, Mary was even more astonished to have Miss Measures' gracious acceptance of the offer. But that was Miss Measures - a lovely lady. Mary and Miss Measures corresponded for some years, but it is not known whether she ever got the ice cream. In fact a later comment recalls that Miss Measures made up some clever mnemonics like '*Dic* had a *duc* with grey *lex*; this is a *fac*'. Joy Pinton has remembered her 'short imperatives' to this day. In today's parlance she was considered to be 'with it'. She married a soldier husband in 1945 and became Marie James. She left the school in 1944.

Miss Ada M.Moss took Geography. She was a strict disciplinarian and became Deputy Head Mistress. Woe betide if you couldn't answer one of her questions' was one summary. Bernice Brookman remembers that 'the first ten minutes of every lesson was spent in her tut-tutting and sighing over the lamentable state of our last homework, and our lack of knowledge'. Miss Moss reprimanded Marian Hale for standing on one leg at a bus stop whilst talking to a boy but for all that Marian liked Miss Moss. Valerie Champion (perhaps over modestly) recalls that when Miss Moss 'told me that I was to be appointed Head Girl she said 'Now Valerie, we don't want you to think you are the best of a bad lot (the notorious 5C) - but I obviously was'. Margaret Lacey laments that 'Miss Moss never liked my work, my general demeanour or my face. She punctuated Geography lessons by making me and the rest of the form aware of this'. Nevertheless, Miss Moss was widely respected - a positive teacher who would always commend work if it was well done - and a most efficient teacher with an interest in world affairs that she shared with many of her older pupils and which went far beyond her own subject. She formed debating teams, encouraging reluctant sixth formers to participate in public debates against other schools in the Town Hall. We know of at least one former pupil who has been eternally grateful for this initiation into public speaking, nerve-wracking though it was at the time. Coming originally from Lancashire, Miss Moss, like Miss Hughes, taught at the school for 36 years, until she retired when the school became comprehensive in 1971. She died only recently.

Miss Nellie White taught biology and inspired Alison Day to read Botany at University, which she did with great success, later becoming involved in penicillin research. Miss White kept bees but one day turned up with her face all swollen, victim of her charges. She taught the rudiments of sex and reproduction 'in rabbits, and even that made her blush' and she 'drooled when she cut up frogs and worms'. Judy Price thought that the immutable friendship between Miss Moss and Miss White seemed so inseparable that in her mind, their subjects of biology and geography became inextricably linked - not exactly helpful apparently in Judy's understanding of either. In fact Miss White and Miss Moss shared a house in Totterdown Road for many years, where Miss Moss continued to live after Miss White died.

Miss Margaret Newman Philips, took Domestic Science. Alison Day recalls that Miss Philips advised them 'to brush their hair 90 times a day'. She pursued the gospel of as little waste as possible and always checked the potato peelings to ensure that every edible scrap had been removed. Joy Pinton remembers making hot water crust pastry that 'would have made a hole in the wall, if you had thrown it at it'. Miss Newman Philips was in charge of the 16th Weston-super-Mare Guide Company which comprised mainly County School girls. Marian Hale recalls Miss Philips as 'being rather shy'. After leaving Weston, she worked in Bath and Cheltenham before retiring in Herefordshire where, only last year (2004) she died, age 94.

Miss Helen Rowe was another mistress who did have a nickname - 'Fishy' Rowe. She was the Art Mistress for much of the early part of the forties. She was the one teacher who from early in the decade taught in both the girls' and the boys' school. I find difficulty with this one. She was more than likely a very talented artist. Kenneth Tucker extols the love of art engendered by Miss Rowe during after-hours Art lessons that she was happy to pursue. But the boys, at least, were beyond her control and many times she disappeared into her room in absolute despair. Alas the notorious girls' form 5C locked her in the cupboard (it was in fact a small anteroom) more than once. As a prefect I was once called in to restore order among the boys and I kept the whole lot in for about an hour after school as a corporate punishment. I do not think that I was among the particularly wayward, but my ability as an artist was absolutely abysmal and I am afraid that I learned nothing during the lessons that I attended. Perhaps it would have been better if we had known her name was Helen.

Miss M. O. Shepherd was the deputy head. She is recalled by Jean Innes as a wonderful maths teacher who never got cross. Valerie Champion recalls her as 'patience personified. She was 'so gentle and kind; we all loved her'. She 'had an aura of quiet authority - very softly spoken, she never had to raise her voice to command attention, or ask for silence'. She was happy to set extra work for the holidays if that was required and Rosemary Sampson recalls being dragged through School Certificate by that means, whilst Jean Ashley thought that with her coaching Miss Shepherd 'performed a miracle' in getting her through School Certificate. Some recall that Miss Shepherd 'had a very tatty gown'.

Miss W. Thompson, took General Science. She was Jean Ashley's form mistress in 2T in 1946. Having been in 1G the year before, her classmates agreed that they would thereafter, always be able to remember how to spell 'Sagittarius'. And so, says Jean, it has proved.

Miss Mary Tracy (known as 'Bunty') arrived in 1946 and taught Domestic Science. She contributed to the Schools 'memories' booklet so we know more about her than some, and one senses that she was part of a new era. Besides teaching, she was responsible for the menus for school dinners, ordering the food and checking the accounts. She also dressed school plays from a very limited budget. Elsewhere we have recorded how Judy Price's love of embroidery was nurtured by Miss Tracy. Miss Tracy became active in the 16th Guide Company. She died in 2004, aged 85.

Miss Upshaw also came later in the decade. My love of art was attributed to Miss Upshaw with whom I spent many happy hours in the art room, recalls Judy Price.

Miss Eveline Webber taught history and is remembered as a 'chirpy, delightful, little person'. She left in 1946

Miss Norah Wight, taught Biology, and conducted 'field trips' in Hutton Woods, which were universally enjoyed. She had nicknames of 'Nellie', 'Smelly Nellie' and 'Aaron'.

So for boys and girls alike, there was a rich range of characters, abilities and idiosyncrasies among those that taught them through those difficult times.

Subject	Term	Exam.	Remarks	Mistress
Scripture	94	86	thoroughly good work.	E.R.B.
English	72	81	Good, Marian works very sensibly.	G.J.
History	67	64	A very pleasing terms work.	wmc.
Geography	69	73	Marian continues to do good work.	Amm.
French	84	80	Very good.	J.M.H.
Latin ~~Chemistry~~	96	85	Very good.	M.H.
Mathematics Arithmetic	73	41	Good on the whole, but examination results are disappointing.	
Algebra	70	49		A.J.
Geometry	60	70		
Gen. Science Biology	68	52	Quite good.	M.C.L.
Domestic Science HYGIENE	71 70	86	Excellent work	M.E.H.
Art	75	63	Good.	K.R.
Physical Training			Good.	D.R.B.

A girls school report embracing many of the staff mentiond above

What follows has a clear connotation to Mr Lindfield, but I'd rather see it as a stand alone and perhaps salutary story of those times. I thus include it, out of all context to the adjoining narrative.

'AUTHORITY - a diversion by Jim Owen.:

My first brush with authority took place soon after I entered the school.

I arrived in the first form with a great friend, Michael Brearley, from Walliscote Road Junior School, in September, 1941. One morning towards the end of my second week I went in search of Michael, whose peg was at the far end of the row. I could see something was wrong. He was sitting shrunk against the wire netting dividing us from the pegs on the other side, oblivious of the noise around him. He turned a tear-stained face to me."Mum's dead," he sobbed. "She died in a car accident last night".

I remember the shock searing through me. At eleven, my mother was part of what any eleven year old took for granted.. I didn't ask what happened. I just sat down numbly by him, I remember the prefect on duty passing by. He stopped, about to tell us to hurry up. Then his expression altered. I blurted out the bad news "You'd better go along with him to the headmaster," he said. "Right away". We walked along the still unfamiliar open walkway beyond our form-room, and turned right, towards the headmaster's office. Mr. Lindfield was standing outside the entrance, watching the school gathering in the form-rooms, his face expressionless.. He looked down at me.

What do YOU want? His tone of voice told me he found the presence of two eleven year olds at this hour of the morning vaguely irregular. I told him what I still couldn't believe. Mr Lindfield looked dispassionately at Michael. "You'd better come into the office," he said and pointed towards the secretary's room. I was reminded of a crow lifting its wing prior to takeoff. "And you", he said after Michael had disappeared. "What are you doing here ? Come to gloat ?

"I remember firing up. Part of it was indignation. I had only done what the prefect said. Part of it was recognition. Something inside me was gloating that my mother was still alive. With all the offended dignity of an eleven year old I replied angrily, "Michael is a friend of mine" and glared back at him. There was a long silence. He looked steadily back at me.

I sensed he was taking in what he was dealing with. A child coming to terms with a tangle of unmanageable emotions. Instead of dealing with my insubordination, he turned away without a word and disappeared into his study. I calmed down. I suppose it was what passed for stress counselling in those days.

Jacksons Faces were the well known promenade photographers. These photos were taken in 1947-1948.

SEGREGATION

If there is one recollection of the schools, shared by just about everybody who went there, it is the segregation of the boys from the girls, and the girls from the boys. The segregation was carried out with almost missionary zeal, not only during school hours but in any circumstance where the schools had some involvement or presence, such as the journey to and from school or at any time in a public place when the school uniform was being worn. Occasionally there were hockey matches between the girls' school's 1st. XI and sixth form boys, but these always had to be held in an aura of secrecy, on the sands.

That the matches might be played on the excellent pitches within the school boundaries, would not have been even worth considering by those who organised those occasions.

As has already been commented upon, the new building, right from the date of its concept, established a rigorous, segregated, two school environment. The anomaly was, of course, that there was both segregation and proximity. Girls and boys travelled on the same buses and the same trains, (but according to the rules, not in the same compartment), they walked to and from the same destinations, they cycled along the same roads. Some boys and girls were brothers and sisters. For some there were the beginnings of relationships. Yet in *all* these circumstances they were expected to retain a separation. It was simply that in the greater school environment they were not meant to be seen together, certainly not in school uniform.

The rigour of this policy does not appear to have been based on any national guide lines, for elsewhere there is ample evidence of more tolerance. At Weston it seems to have been largely down to the standards set by the headmistress and the headmaster. In the case of the girls it was Miss Farthing. We have talked of Miss Farthing elsewhere, but this formidable lady had an uncompromising attitude when it came to any association of her girls, with boys. It simply was not on. Both Mr Lindfield and Mr Price supported this policy and their own rather aloof demeanour suggested that they might well be active sympathisers, yet one wonders if they in turn were not overawed by Miss Farthing.

The segregationist policy took a battering, as we shall see, when both schools had to occupy the boys' half, following the air raid. What had been a rigorous north-south divide, had to be converted into a far more fragile east-west divide. In the original configuration you need never, perhaps even could never, see a member of the opposite sex, on the school premises. Now there were crossing places (the corridor outside the boys' hall was a classic), where you might be held up whilst the opposite sex were ushered past. One sex would never infiltrate the passing of the other sex, but always let them pass first. The teachers made sure of that. One boy pupil has commented that the level of ignorance of the facts of life among his peers, was quite incredible - but *he* knew them! He says that he found himself often addressing this problem for the benefit of his fellows on such occasions, whilst queuing to let the girls go by. To this day he remains uncertain whether he was considered to be helpful, or just a 'dirty little boy'.

The opposite sex were now to be seen just the other side of the quadrangle and a seat on that side of the form room was at a premium. Interest wasn't all one sided - 'the shock of the bombing of the girls school was ameliorated by the fact that we would be able to see the boys' one girl pupil of those times, has recently written. Furthermore, the *other* side of the girls' classroom looked out on to the boys playing fields. The other side of the *boys'* classroom looked on to the (boys') bicycle sheds. Little is fair, in this world. Some parts of the building were used by both schools - the boys' Physics and Chemistry labs, were cases in point. This gave opportunity, as Betty Page has recalled, 'to leave sneeky little notes for fancied adolescent boys'.

Sometimes segregation held by the thickness of a door. The original medical room (which seemed to straddle both schools) was commandeered by the girls as a 6th form common room. However, the small ante-room associated with it, remained as part of the boys' school. The door between them was firmly locked and the door handle removed. The resulting hole in the door then became an aperture for squirting a water pistol from the boys side to the girls side, acknowledged later as a crass and immature venture. For a while the two boy occupants held sway, but then the girls summoned up a garden syringe and near flooded the boys out. Unconditional surrender was the boys' lot The lot of the ante room duo did not appear to improve when they were actually correctly ensconced on the girls side of the door. On one occasion a mixed 6th form class were left on their own to read a Shakespeare play in this girls 6th form common room. It was in an environment in which, by the boys' own admission, the girls were mature, and the boys anything but. Something or other led to one of the girls flinging a book at Roy Perry which hit him right on the bridge of his nose, breaking his glasses. He had to cycle home to get another pair.

The arrival of the US Army in Weston-super-Mare, must have sent Miss Farthing into paroxysms of concern. Mary Price recalls that Miss Farthing circulated all parents with a letter warning them against allowing their daughters to go to 'grown-up dances where G.I's might be present'. Perhaps to head off such trouble, Mary recalls that a dance was organised in the school hall for 5th and 6th formers, but one truly wonders how many 5th and 6th form boys could actually dance. Mary's abiding recollection however is of the girls rubbing off the lipstick which they had dared to apply. Perhaps, in truth, a new era was beginning to emerge, for on Thursday 15th February 1945, there was a combined party for the *first* forms of both schools, an event meriting a mention in the school magazine. It was actually repeated a year later but not carried on to the second formers, a risk assessment probably having indicated that the alarm bells were ringing. I do not recall being involved in any combined social activity, organised on the school premises, up to the time that I left in 1948.

Later Miss Farthing's flank was turned by the presence of 'strapping young men' who arrived to rebuild the school. My girl school informant tells me that 'one of our girls arranged a date with a builder and became most disappointed when he turned up in a very sharp suit and hair slicked back - not at all like his 'tarzan' appearance on the school site'. Naturally the story was of told of a third party - they always are.

There was no sex education - certainly not for the boys. Paul Warren confirms this and goes on, "I remember once being in a small bunch of second formers gathered agog around a sixth former, while he explained 'what you do is you put your hand inside the girls blouse'. I thought he was very advanced". It was Jean Innes who remembered 'how Miss White had her work cut out explaining to a mostly embarrassed and giggling class of girls, the rudiments of sex and reproduction' - *of rabbits*, (a contemporary, and early proof reader of these notes, has added).

Eventually, matters took a more serious line. Derek Porter has written of how he was called into the presence of Mr Price, and told that as Head Boy he had to conform with the rules and thus stop cycling to school with 'a girl'. He was given 24 hours to consider his position. Derek thought the rule ridiculous and found support in his fellow prefects. He confronted Mr Price next day with the potential resignations of them all, which led to Mr Price backing down. Thereafter the rules about fraternisation were slowly relaxed. Derek and 'the girl' - Barbara Morrill - were married for over fifty years, before Barbara died in January 2005.

Of course all this was within the confines of the school and its extended authority. Beyond that, most girl-boy friendships of those who attended the school were indeed *between* pupils of the school. The Scout/Guide link was quite a strong one, the daily bus and train journey for many, was another, coming across each other in the High Street on a Saturday morning was yet another and at Christmas time, parties in private houses, albeit pretty innocent, were very common. Fortes Ice Cream Parlour was as near as we got to clubbing but it played its part. The whole era established a surprising number of stable marriages between pupils, that have survived to this day.

Perhaps growing up very slowly had its long term rewards.

THE CATCHMENT AREA AND TRAVELLING.

It is no longer clear if the school had, or was allocated, a fixed catchment area. However for the original Nithsdale Road school its 'catchment' embraced Yatton to the north, Axbridge to the east and Highbridge to the south, and that area was probably maintained for the new school. Certainly, pupils did travel by train from Clevedon and Yatton in the north, and from Highbridge in the south. Pupils came by bus, certainly from Sand Bay (No 153), Blagdon, Sandford, Churchill, Banwell and Hutton (Nos 43 and 44) and Burnham-on-Sea, Brent Knoll and Bleadon (No 42) and from other places *en route*. Because of the constraints placed by public service time tables and the realities of distance, train and bus girls and boys seemed at the time to have a certain separate presence, in the way of things at the school. During the era of sharing the school with the evacuees for instance, two (Weston) boys in each class were allocated the task of cleaning their classroom at the end of the morning to facilitate a quick turn round for the afternoon shift. In questioning the origin of this concept, one form commented rather testily 'anyone would think it was the bus and train contingent [who originated the idea], to judge from their exemption from this duty'. Thus although not in a particularly offensive way, the travellers tended to be labelled and known as, 'train girls', 'train boys' etc.,etc. They, in turn, had a certain camaraderie. It was always a matter of perception. One pupil who lived in Worle recalls that his mother always called pupils who lived in metropolitan Weston as 'town boys'. It seemed that a tuppeny bus ride separated town from country.

Of course this journeying could take quite a time and pupils from Clevedon, say, could be away from home for about 10 hours every weekday. At the outset, when Dave Edwards started at the school in 1936, he cycled from Blagdon to Churchill Gate (about 3 miles) and then caught a bus to Weston - another 10 hour day. The bus company later put on a bus all the way to Blagdon making things a bit easier, and indeed increasing the number or pupils who came to the County School from the Blagdon area. In truth if there was a defined catchment area, practicalities sometimes undermined it. One wonders how many incoming pupils met Westonians going the other way. Certainly, Marian Hale's brother Alan who passed the scholarship from Locking Road School like his two sisters before him and later, his younger brother after him, could not be found a place at Weston in 1946 and had to travel daily to Dr. Morgan's School at Bridgwater - another ten hour day. His three siblings (June, Marian and Roger) all went to the County School.

In the normal way of affairs the school pupils were issued with season tickets for the train and their bus fares were paid for, or reimbursed. However there was a certain parsimony in its implementation, for the main departure train back to Yatton and Clevedon left Weston at 4.35 pm and school finished at 3.50 pm. The authorities deemed that this left sufficient time to walk to the station, and thus bus fares were not reimbursed for that journey - a distance of about 1¾ miles. Time being of the essence, the morning bus fare *was* paid for.

A surprising aspect of the war years was the utter reliability of the bus service, certainly of the Weston urban services and probably the country services as well. Bus routes and numbers seemed almost cast in stone. Most of the urban services would have carried pupils on some part of their journey to school. They were all public services - not specifically *school* buses. The double deck service No 40, Worle to Moorland Road was a core route for many, although it involved a short walk at the Moorland Road end to get to Broadoak Road. The single deck, double entry (well one was exit only), No 90, terminated at Broadoak Road having come from Worlebury, whose hill probably dictated the single-deck configuration. The double deck 163 came from the Old Pier, along Beach Road, pass the school and on to Uphill, whilst the 152 paralleled that route for part of the way. The other principal east-west route, was the double deck 154 serving Locking Road, using Baytree Road and the Grand Pier as its destinations. Then there were the rather dinky little Dennis chassis'd 93 (Railway Station to Flagstaff Hill, up in the Shrubbery) and 153 (Railway Station to Sand Bay via Worle and Kewstoke). All served us well and the only remaining bonus was to get a bus ticket whose four figure serial number added up to twenty-one. If you got one of those you thought that it was going to be your lucky day (but it never was).

There was apparently a thing called a 'scholar's demand ticket' which permitted travel on the buses at a child's rate until 16, as opposed to the normal adult fare charge which generally applied from the age of 14, the normal secondary school leaving age until 1945. My recollections are that reimbursement for journeys within the immediate Weston area only applied to one-way journeys of over 3 route-miles, they were paid in arrears and Bill Davies was the arbiter of eligibility, for the boys. Children's fares were typically 1d. 1½d and 2d., the latter sufficient to take your from Worle to Moorland Road - the total route of the No 40.

Compared with what you see today, pupil behaviour on public transport, particularly on the buses was quite decorous. It couldn't always be said of the train boys (and girls), who were probably the biggest group not under the regular surveillance of school staff. If there was a request from the school stage that 'train' boys should remain after the rest had been dismissed, it usually meant a strong reprimand for misbehaviours reported by train staff or the general public. Notionally, boys and girls were supposed to travel in separate compartments in the last two carriages of the train but monitors appointed to achieve this aim, had an impossible task. One gets the impression that the trackside must have been littered with caps and hats lost out of the windows going by the number of people who have reported being admonished for that default.

Pupils, indeed most children of that era, would give up their seat to an adult who was standing. The wartime emergency regulation that six people must form a queue was widely accepted and most embarkation on the buses was done in a civil manner.

But for all the bus and train travel, cycling was probably the majority method of coming to school. Traffic in those days of course was a fraction of what it is now, and the principal hazards mainly came from the weather. Weston could be a very windy place indeed and cycling against a south-westerly gale along the sea front, let alone the other main routes, could be quite a challenge. Yet the fitness that it engendered seemed to stay with us for many years to come. With the wind *behind* you, you could achieve somewhat hazardous speeds. The principal device to combat pouring rain was the oilskin cape. I suppose that it *was* impervious and one was fit enough not to perspire too much, but my core recollection is of always arriving at school quite dry.

The law of the land was regularly enforced and two-on-a-bike, riding without lights, even *pushing* your cycle in the wrong direction up the one-way High Street and certainly riding on the pavement, could all, as a minimum, incur some type of formal admonishment and often a fine. The school itself (I don't think that it was against the law) railed against riding more than two abreast, mainly because of the impact that such a practice had on other road users. School uniform, and thus the school hat or cap had to be worn on all these comings and goings, so that this minor example of anti-social behaviour would have been deemed to reflect adversely on the school. There was also the all pervading requirement that boys and girls from the school should not cycle in each others company.

Double decker buses provided something of a wind shield against a prevailing gale and tagging on behind one of them, particularly along the sea front was not uncommon. Of course when the bus stopped, you stopped and waited for the people to get on and off. This was not a very intelligent practice for all sorts of reasons and was frowned on by the school, but it was, alas, quite common. On one such occasion (it was the 23rd October '45) two of us were sheltering behind a stationary 163 along the Beach Road waiting for the bus to move off. It was going southbound, somewhere near the onetime 'Allendale' nursing home. A younger pupil (Hoon) was cycling hard, head down against the wind and didn't notice the stationary bus. Suddenly, bang!.... and there he was, a crumpled heap between us. I can't remember the details after that, but I know I went to the hospital with him - he was only concussed - and I do remember that the hospital got me to ring his mother to tell her what had happened, a task that I did not relish.

And of course there were quite a number of pupils who walked to school, but I can recall no occasion when a pupil was driven to school in the all too rare car of a parent.

DISCIPLINE AND BEHAVIOUR

The Boys.

It is probably in the area of discipline and behaviour that most will probably feel there has been the greatest changes since the 1940s. There certainly was discipline in the 1940s, but much of it was self-imposed and accepted as being the norm for the age. Behaviour followed within the constraints imposed by the discipline, but the pupils were very far from cowed and some of the initiatives to reflect that, were really quite imaginative. But there seems no evidence of any viciousness in the schools and no one has talked of any bullying, indeed Ivan Armstrong has commented that 'school life developed a great deal of camaraderie in the form, which was quite new for me'. Although sport was a major component of school life, not everyone showed prowess and someone has commented that 'that didn't form any sort of barrier nor any feelings of condescension' between members of the classroom. The

Scouts often went to school in uniform on Fridays, with sheath knives on their belts or down their stockings, but the notion that they might stab one or other of their fellows, would have been considered a very bizarre concept indeed. Nowadays they seem to talk of metal detectors in schools, to discourage homicide by knife wielding pupils.

Graham Venn has summarised the discipline regime as a rising degree of sanctions. First of all was the return of unsatisfactory work to be done again after school hours. Then came mild physical correction, a piece of chalk or even a blackboard rubber might come winging your way if you were inattentive. This was normally the prerogative of a small number of teachers. Then there were 'lines', of the 'I must not talk in class' sort, to be written a hundred times say, in the miscreant's own time. Then there was detention, the requirement to attend school, sometimes on a Saturday morning and sometimes on a Monday after normal school hours. It was for about an hour during which time the detainee had to write an essay, or write more 'lines'. Any problem that followed from having to attend a detention at the stipulated hour was for the pupil to resolve not the school. Most misdemeanours were met by these sanctions, which were mainly administered by the prefects. The causal event and the sanction were largely transient happenings, and although recorded, this was largely to ensure that the sanction had been administered.

Serious breaches of discipline for the boys could be met by the cane, administered only by the headmaster, and considered within the school regime to be a very definite blot on (and entry in) the copybook. What few accounts or recollections of caning that survive talk generally of two or three strokes but sometimes four, on the hand or on the bottom. It could be quite painful, but it seems to have been a *fairly* rarely used event. Nevertheless it was a sanction that was readily and uncontroversially available.

The final sanction was expulsion, probably entirely at the discretion of the headmaster. I cannot remember a permanent expulsion being enacted whilst I was at the school, and so the issues that it raised never surfaced. However, I do think that there might have been a near miss if rumours were to be believed. One mid school pupil who somehow managed to be excused cross-country, chose to have a go at the runners with a catapult. This would have been considered a heinous offence. His expulsion was assumed by everyone. However suddenly a grand piano appeared in the hall and this was generally assumed to be blood money paid by his parents. He certainly stayed on at the school. I feel that there is some truth in this but I could not be absolutely sure. No names.

There were also random sanctions like being told to pick up paper in the quadrangle, for 'looking at the girls'.

Detentions were commonplace, not handed out willy-nilly, but a standard hazard for the minor miscreant. Running within the school building, being caught in a public place without your cap, late for school too many times, even too boisterous play could result in a detention. Teachers could give them for indiscipline in the classroom. The miscreant would be told at the time and his name would then be entered into the 'detention book'. The detention book was taken around the classrooms on a Friday afternoon when detention slips would be handed out to the miscreants. I remember that once when I was giving out the detentions, form 2b were having a French lesson. Each detention recipient would acknowledge his name with a strong, fairly cheeky and rather overstated 'oui!'. One chap however had to acknowledge two detentions and he did this with a very vernacular driven 'wee wee!'. You had to laugh.

After the detentions were handed out a senior prefect took the detention book to the Head Master, a task disliked by Roy Perry in taking the book to 'Tiny' Price, for Price seldom said a word. Adrian Lunnon seems to recall that the detention cards were in one of two colours - one colour for the teachers' detentions and one for the prefects'.

Accounts of canings, perhaps not surprisingly are quite rare. Leonard Reeves has written of the day that he and four others skipped a gardening session and nipped out from school. They ran headlong into the headmaster. This merited visits to the headmaster's study where two strokes of the cane on the buttocks were administered. 'You could hear the swish of the cane and an abrupt thwack while waiting in the corridor outside the study' he relates.

Trevor Rowsell is another informant. He was among a group of pupils who, for devilment, were mixing chemicals in the Chemistry Lab, willy-nilly. Just as Curly Hay appeared, this random mixture gave off an impressive white cloud. Curley demanded the name(s) of the activists but no one would own up. Eventually Trevor volunteered his name. Trevor thought Curley a 'nice chap' so was somewhat aghast when Curley directed him to the headmasters study. There he expressed his guilt to Mr Lindfield but this didn't save him from three whacks across the hand. However in amelioration perhaps for owning up, Mr Lindfield said that no record would be made or kept of this punishment.

Gus Fletcher recalls four strokes on the buttocks. He, alas, had been smoking on the Yatton-Weston train when to his misfortune, H. C. Wood who by chance was catching the same train onwards to address a family problem, caught him extinguishing his cigarette. Gus waited in some apprehension for the return of Mr Wood but the day came, the report was made, and Gus was called into the presence of Tiny Price. Mr Price explained what the punishment would be and offered, or was it threatened, to call in Mr Bill Davies to help Gus to stand up to the punishment. Gus was stoic and declined the offer. But it was painful and Gus remembers that Mrs Dowding kept a cushion on a chair in the kitchen to assist in the acceptance of the initial pain and discomfort. Gus half remembers that Mrs Dowdell gave him a cup of Bovril.

There were, no doubt, other resorts to the cane to address passing defaults of a serious nature. None of these punishments - real or threatened - seem to have any effect on the spirit or liveliness of the school. It was the norm and it no doubt bought about some inner discipline.

The cupboards at the back of the classrooms offered a certain scope for a bit of private initiative. Again we are indebted to Trevor Rowsell. He recalls how two of his form colleagues decided to sit out a whole lesson in one of these cupboards. One fellow sat on the floor the other on a mid-height shelf. It was in one of 'Sherlock' Holmes maths lessons. However the door started to open and a hand appeared from within to close it. Mr Holmes noticed that and the perpetrators were hauled out. Holmes gave them both detentions, but by the end of the lesson he had withdrawn them, with the observation 'it needed courage to do that'.

Chris Roberts is another person whose penchant for the cupboard is remembered by many. He decided to sit out a lesson in the cupboard but succumbed to a bout of cramp, and fell out. Alas, his aftermath was more serious; he was suspended until the end of term, which included participation in the 'mock Oxfords' - the trial run for the School Certificate to be taken the following term. However he found a job as a life guard at the 'Pool' and waved to the rest of us as we wended our way to school. A few years later whilst pursuing this lifeguard role as a holiday job, he was interviewed by Richard Dimbleby, on the 'Down Your Way' programme, and thus gained a short lived fame. He chose Litolff's *Scherzo*, played by Dame Moura Lympany for his record. It was perhaps rather bizarre that Chris Roberts lost his life whilst bathing in Florida in May 1997.

Cupboards clearly have their attractions.

The surviving door windows seemed to be victims of continued damage - contrived or by accident. A heavily laden satchel could tip over a chair and if this collided with the glass, there was but one result. Sometimes this was contrived by passing a number of satchels quietly forward to hang over the leading chair, unknown to its sitter. When he stood up, over went the chair and bingo - a smashed window. In truth *I* really do not remember these forays into the crazy, and although others can vouch for them I really do not think that they were anywhere near the norm. Yet, quite early on, there was a comment in a fifth form report in the school magazine that 'The approach of school certificate has had other strange results. We have become so quiet and dignified that not a single window has been broken in our room'. In a P.S. to their 1940 report, Form III(2) reported that they 'had not broken a single window all summer term'. But in the same edition of the school magazine was a very funny (and clever) poem, which commenced,

> *The boy stood by the broken pane,*
> *Whence all but he had fled,*
> *To hide his deed he knew was vain,*
> *The glass all round was spread'.*

The poem continues on how he had to pay a five shillings damage fee, which meant that the broken glass was nothing compared with his broken heart.

Another ruse was to lock all the doors from within and then set the final window bolt so that it fell into place as you shut the door - the whole room seemingly locked from within. A caretaker's despair.

Michael Gates recalls that when they were in a second form physics lesson they learned about the 'force gun'. Details now appear scant. Their classroom at that time was the school hall and he remembers how with the knowledge gained, someone in the class managed to get a blob of ink on the hall ceiling. It *was*, after all, quite high. He additionally recalls that if he sensed a misdemeanour, Mr Pinton would call out 'Steadfast!' as he entered the hall. It would appear that everyone then had to freeze whilst any default was unearthed. One default that wasn't unearthed in time, was when Mr Pinton was deputising for Mr Thomas as the pianist at morning assembly. He couldn't get a note out of the piano, not surprising really, given that the piano was full of small milk bottles.

Another minor distraction arose from a thing called 'Fletcher's Trolley' This was a bit of equipment in the Physics' Lab, which could leave a trace from an oscillating pen, as it accelerated under the influence of a suspended weight. This device normally rested on the bench at the back of the room. One form contrived to tie a long cotton from it, around the gas taps and into the hands of one of the class sitting near the front. He could cause the trolley to start moving, seemingly of its own volition and to the theoretical surprise, and hopefully to the consternation, of the Physics master. This was a well known story, contemporary at the time, but I am hard put to say that it actually happened.

At a more erudite level we have 'Nip' Watts's dismissal of a message from 'Speedy' Harris. Mr Harris was trying to concentrate the minds of his Mathematics class, in form 5a, which seemed relatively disinterested in the fact that the Oxford School Certificate examinations were only a few weeks away. He was promoting the need for perseverance and commitment. It was May 1945 and Mr Winston Churchill was at the height of his fame. 'How do you think Mr Churchill got to where he is today?' thundered Mr Harris, a question he thought permitted but one answer. Most of the class would have been prepared to leave it at that, but not 'Nip' Watts. With an authoritative nonchalance he volunteered 'because he is the son of Lord Randolph Churchill'. Mr Harris nearly had apoplexy at the dismissal of what he saw as such a powerful message.

Discipline didn't seem to be at the expense of spirit

The Girls

Perhaps as one would expect, at least for those times, the girls code of discipline was somewhat easier, with the ultimate sanction of caning, off the menu. Elsewhere in the land, caning of girls was indeed still carried out. However there were detentions and there was the concept of 'order marks'. These 'order marks' were given against certain minor misdemeanours such as talking in class or reading girls' magazines in class. Mary Price was mortified when she was given an order mark on her very first day. In her excitement she had left her gas mask at home. The term's total was recorded on the individuals end-of-term report. During her very first week at the shared school Judy Price, somewhat lost, 'wandered further into the male environment than was considered appropriate' and was given a 'double order mark'. Recollection of what followed this award of order marks isn't too clear, but the general consensus appears to be that if you amassed three, perhaps within a certain time span, the defaulter had to appear in front of Miss Farthing. Order marks were also the likely basis for any comment on the girl's behaviour, in the end-of-term report.

Marian Hale recalls 'breaking three school rules in one fell swoop'. She was reprimanded by Miss Moss (who Marian much respected) for being at a bus stop outside the school, not wearing her hat (one default), standing on one leg and thus in an unladylike fashion, (second default), and talking to a boy (third default). However, I think that she only got a verbal admonishment.

To be called into the presence of Miss Farthing, was an invitation that most approached with a certain dread. A common consensus, even among those who have subsequently proved themselves to be quite worldly, was that they went to her presence 'in fear and trembling'. The simple command 'come' in response to a knock on her door turned legs to jelly. If the offence was serious enough, the parents were also asked to visit Miss Farthing to ensure that there was no misunderstanding, relating to Miss Farthing's concerns about the errant pupil. 'Consorting with boys' was a fairly common indictment. June (sister of Marian) Hale's mother was so summoned when June left notes for the Barking Abbey boys as related on page 33. Another

Surprisingly, pole dancing was not on the school curriculum, but Polly Price thought that she should give it a go, before deciding eventually for the Civil Service.

parent was called to Miss Farthing's presence because the pupil, with her family, had gone to the cinema on the Friday evening and to the theatre on the Saturday. 'One evening socialising was enough' the parent was told. The parent on this occasion contested that assertion!

But the girls weren't little angels. Oh, no. I leave it to Mary Price to recall one situation.

"We were a lively group and needed firm handling and I cannot remember anyone taking us aside and explaining how much distress we were causing the inexperienced staff. We were told that the staff would not teach us for two weeks. We chose the best *students* to 'teach' us and

I remember looking up and seeing two staff members watching us 'at work'. They were obviously amused. We had one of the best School Certificate results that the school had achieved. When I went to work at the local education office I found out that one of the girls' parents had challenged the legality of the school's refusing to teach us."

On the whole, though, as one past pupil has acknowledged, 'we were a pretty compliant bunch of girls'.

Thus for the boys and for the girls there was a code of discipline and punishment, understood by all.

SUBJECTS

When remembering all the vicissitudes of the war (as we will), of the travelling and the girl-boy (boy-girl) distractions, it is quite easy to forget that we actually went to the school to learn, or at least to have lessons, and to put it simply, to be tested thereon. The overall arbiter of what we were taught were the requirements of the two public examinations that dominated the schools' academic environment at that time - the Oxford School Certificate and the Bristol Higher School Certificate. It was the pupil's responsibility to learn, not to question. Most of the subjects taught are named in the mention of the staff, in an earlier chapter. Thus the core curriculum embraced mathematics - arithmetic, algebra, geometry and trigonometry (but not necessarily all four), English language, English literature, History, Geography, Latin (which could be dropped in the third form by the boys and in the fourth form by the girls, in favour of chemistry), French (the only modern foreign language on offer), some combination of Physics, Chemistry, Biology and General Science (I think that you took any three out of the four), then a discretionary Art and/or a discretionary Handicraft (principally woodwork) for the boys and Domestic Science for the girls. Scripture featured as an examined subject in the junior school but after that, it seemed to settle for a one word summary in the end-of-term report - typically, 'satisfactory' - if at all. There was regular, quite rigorously monitored, homework in all the academic subjects; so commonplace was it that no one has even mentioned it.

It is difficult to summarise the level of expected attainment in all these subjects but the Oxford School Certificate examination papers for 1941 which form an appendix to these recollections, gives some idea of that expectation along with some idea of the scope of the core syllabus. Inevitably one thinks of how current pupils might address this examination, it being the sole arbiter (other than in some vocational subjects) as to whether you passed or failed. There was no examined course work. You won or lost on the day.

Judy Price has written that her love of embroidery was first nurtured by the Domestic Science mistress (Miss Tracy). 'We were required to make cookery caps and aprons, each embroidered with our initials, in the school colours. The general idea was to teach us every stitch in the book in that one project, hemming, making pockets, attaching tape and elastic, sewing on facings, and finally embroidery. Both cap and apron were thoroughly uncomfortable but only thus attired were any of us allowed near the cookery room'. In that cookery room Judy learned the 'correct proportions of fat and flour and the gentle art of soup making, producing the most revolting mixtures which we were meant to carry home' For Judy this meant a bus to the station, a ten mile train ride and a fifteen minute walk. A pot of soup was not an ideal travelling companion.

Throughout the school life, all subjects were tested at the end of most terms, marks given for both the term and the examination achievements, and a final class position given. Modern educationalists would no doubt tear their hair out at what they would see as this blatant expression of relative inferiority/superiority, but which I, along with others at the time, found to be an incentive to try to do better. These results, along with disciplinary defaults, were all recorded in a hard covered report book which had to be signed by the parent and returned on the first day of the new term. The prestige of this process was slightly undermined by 'Algebra' being spelt incorrectly (Alegebra) in all the girls report books printed to replace those burned in the air raid of June 1942, and were thus in use for many years.

The report book also contained a loose sheet which required at the beginning of each term, the parent to assert that their child had not ' been exposed to any infectious or contagious illness during the past six weeks'.

RELIGIOUS INSTRUCTION.

We were, I suppose, what we would now call mono-cultural. Very few would have been exposed to other cultures or other beliefs. As far as I can recall, we were all white, and with the rarest exception, nominally Christian. After all, in those days our first names were always known as our *Christian* names. But even then, the range of *true* Christian conviction probably spanned a wide spectrum.

Thus there was a general presumption, undoubtedly correct, that this Christian orientation was the starting point for any religious instruction or for any corporate acts of reflection, or of thanks, or of remembrance.

Both schools started off the day with their school gathered in assembly, with most of the staff there, for a lesson read from the Bible and the singing of a hymn. Roy Perry seems to recall Mr Price using the same Collect over and over again, along the lines of 'O Lord who has safely brought us to the beginning of another day, defend us in the same with thy mighty spirit....'

More prosaically, I recall that when a Royal Navy ship was sunk, we sang with some feeling,

> *Eternal Father, strong to save*
> *Whose arm hath bound the restless wave,*
> *Who biddest the mighty ocean deep,*
> *Its own appointed limits keep,*
> *Oh, hear us when we cry to Thee*
> *For those in peril on the sea',*

I can hear it now. For many, I think that religious observances offered a certain solace for the war.

At more formal school events, typically on Speech Day, the boys sang the school hymn,

> *Where is thy God, my soul?*
> *Is He within thy heart;*
> *Or ruler of a distant realm*
> *In which thou hast no part?*

For the girls, the morning hymn was chosen by the senior classes in turn, often accompanied on the piano by a musically capable pupil. Marian Hale's form for instance, favoured 'For all the Saints who from their labours rest'. Sometimes Mr. Thomas, the music master played the piano for their assembly, and his boisterous rendering of 'Men of Harlech' to see them out of the hall occasionally clashed with a quiet moment in the adjoining boys' assembly.

However to my request for recollections, Kenneth F. Tucker responded with some angst. 'You ask about religion. Well, of course, in our day we were indoctrinated at school (no political correctness then) in the Christian religion........As the pressure of work and study eased I began reading anthropology, archaeology and the like which made me see Christianity in a totally different light......I suppose that I am now a Pagan..' Denis Hawkings on the other was actually surprised (in a comparison sense) at the paucity of religious instruction, at only one lesson per week. His elementary school had been Worle CofE school where there was an a hours scripture lesson before anything else started, every day.

There doesn't seem a lot to support Kenneth Tucker's view. However, on the occasion of the Boys' Speech Day on 18th December 1940, the main address was given by Rev. Preb. A. Chisholm, Rector of the Parish Church. He didn't mince his words. He said *'..[it is] not sufficient merely to train men to be good citizens, according to any standard of citizenship. We must aim at nothing less than the training of Christian citizens'*. Since then, things have changed so much that such sentiments expressed at a state school would now probably not see him invited back.

A page from Margaret England's Scripture Exercise Book.

In contrast, I find that my recollection is that formal religious instruction was fairly fragmented and mild. As detailed in the earlier section on the boys' staff, at the outset of the decade the school staff included Mr J.G.(Sherlock) Holmes, who had taught Maths and Scripture since 1925, and whose general humanity was widely admired. He was ordained as a priest at a ceremony at Wells Cathedral on 22nd September 1940, but left the school in July 1943 to become a Chaplain in the Royal Navy Volunteer Reserve. Thereafter the role of religious instruction seemed to fall largely on the Headmaster, Mr 'Tiny' Price. Paul Warren recalls Mr. Price taking the fifth form. Mr Price said that he would equip his audience to combat those that they would eventually meet who would tell them that their Christian beliefs were untrue. He would tell us, during the

year, both sides of the argument on various points. ' I do not remember his individual points, but I do remember listening with interest to his lessons, but feeling that the arguments against, were the stronger. The result was that I had lost my Christian faith by the end of the year.' concludes Paul, perhaps a little sadly. A salutary tale. Trevor Rowsell recalls with some precision, that as he was cycling past the Bus Station on Beach Road, he suddenly thought 'if I *do* go to hell, so what?'.

For others it was the beginning of a vocation that was to dominate their lives. Among my immediate friends Roy Peacock became a Minister in the Methodist Church and Denis Hodge, after some years as a general practitioner became an ordained minister in the Church of England.

Roy in his book 'A Peacock's Tale' relates his progress and increasing responsibility in his Church, culminating in the superintendancy of Callington and Gunnislake in Cornwall, a responsibility embracing fifteen churches.

Denis became a Bishop in the Anglo-Catholic Church, in New Zealand in 1993. His awakening seemed a little unusual. He recalls that 'Don Mather [a postwar arrival to teach mainly English] was to teach us 'Scripture'. The pile of Bibles under his arm were ceremoniously dumped in favour of 'ethics' which was, and remains, a euphemism for liberalisation. These persuaded me to look more carefully into the scriptures he so readily abandoned. Not the only influence, of course, but I have asked myself just how influential he was in the rest of my career.'

On 29th September 1943 a joint, girls' and boys' Commemoration Service was inaugurated as an annual event. It was held at the Weston Parish Church. Miss Farthing, explained that this was an initiative of Mr Price which she was most happy to support. 'Being state schools we have neither Patron nor illustrious founder' she commented, a circumstance that the Commemoration Service would address; 'another landscape in the school life'. In January 1946 another new initiative was the convening of a conference in conjunction with the Student Christian Movement in Schools, which about fifty girls and boys from the Vth and VIth forms attended.

The girls do not seem to remember much about any formal religious instruction save the subject of 'Scripture' in the earlier years. This did not seem to be in the form of any rigorous, or any, indoctrination into the Christian religion, but more a study of the biblical story. There was always the morning assembly with a hymn and a lesson, and at the end of term, Miss Farthing always read the parable of the talents. For the more senior girls Miss Farthing carried forward the Scripture lessons.

Marian Hale remembers that in one lesson Miss Farthing went through all the plagues of Egypt as related in Exodus and gave a natural, as opposed to the supernatural, explanation. It was a revelation to Marian that 'one did not have to accept everything in the bible as a literal truth' a concept with which she already had, problems. 'For this healthy scepticism I owe her my thanks'.

SCHOOL UNIFORM

The girls and the boys both had a school uniform. Other secondary schools in the state sector did not normally have a uniform and thus this circumstance reflected a measure of elitism as seen by the school's detractors, but as an irksome imposition by a minority of those who had to wear it - particularly the head gear. The majority however did get pleasure from its visible evidence that you 'went to the County School'. In those years Weston had a large number of private schools of varying merit, and these always had some form of identifying uniform.

The County Schools' requirements, were not relaxed in any significant way even on the advent of clothes rationing in 1941.

For the girls, Margaret England has written that 'we wore modern tailored, navy blue pinafore dresses, white blouse and a tie, black stockings, blazer and velour hat in winter, and blue and white cotton dresses, white ankle socks and straw hat [panama] in summer. We wore a pale blue Grecian style dress, and matching knickers for gym'. The school tie was in maroon and yellow. Jean Innes recalls that the gym dresses 'were very brief for ease of movement, and we felt quite daring in them'. Summer dresses were made of blue cotton material with white lines making a squared pattern. This material was purchased in a local store and was usually made up by a mother or a dressmaker. A certain leeway was allowed but dresses were supposed to have a white collar and the short sleeves had to have a white cuff. Save for the hat this regime seemed to survive throughout the war. Janet Lovell (Owen) however does comment that as the war wore on the blue serge tunics became blue skirts and white blouses. Skirts were officially permitted in the sixth form. Mary Ashley has written that 'we liked our school uniform, but used to contort our hats into weird shapes to be more glamorous. Strangely we had to kneel down to have our summer dresses fitted and the hems had to be six inches above the knee'. This recollection comes as a surprise to others. Mary Price recalls that 'I hardly ever went without my blazer because I had two dresses made into one, with a dropped waistline - not school uniform!'

The boys sartorial complement does not appear to have been so well recorded by any male contemporaries, but Wm. Burrow Ltd. in Meadow Street, one of the school's appointed outfitters, advertised 'Hard Wearing Clothing for the School Boy. The 'County School' [grey?] tweed knicker suit in all sizes'. They went on, to offer, 'County School' shirts with two detached collars, in white and [or?] grey.' In the days before washing machines everyday clothing was worn for much longer periods and 'two detached collars' probably saw the shirt itself being worn for the best part of a week. There was, of course, a school tie. But above all this, sat the school cap, a source of pride in some (Ivan Armstrong was admonished for wearing his before he actually joined the school, so proud of it was he) but seen as an imposition by authority, by others, particularly as they got older. It was also a sign of seniority in the form that it could take. The basic hat was a red cap with a yellow hoop with, initially, a metal badge at the front. Detractors from other local schools would sometimes call out, 'Strawberries and Cream' in reference to the County School cap. On entering the sixth form, the cap went to plain black with the badge, and on being made a prefect, a tassel was added to the crown. This hat, with a tassel, could be and often was worn with a certain panache. The school hat had to be worn at all times in any public place, and one was expected to touch your cap, by way of a modest salute, if you came across a member of staff in the street.

COMPLETE SCHOOL OUTFITS

OUTFITTERS BY APPOINTMENT TO THE COUNTY SCHOOL.

HARD WEARING CLOTHING FOR THE SCHOOL BOY.

The "County School" Tweed Knicker Suit at 29/11 in all sizes. As recommended.

"County School" Shirts with two detached collars, in white and grey, priced at 4/6 and 5/6.

Guaranteed for Wear. Made specially for the County School boy. School House Shoes in all sizes.

COMPLETE FOOTBALL & GYM OUTFITS IN STOCK.

EVERYTHING for the SCHOOL BOY

Wm. BURROW LTD.

MEADOW STREET :: Weston-super-Mare

Weston-super-Mare Gazette, Ltd.

Both schools, at the outset of the era, required what were known as 'house shoes', which had elastic inserts, to be worn whilst on the school premises. Outdoor shoes were not to be worn in school, and each pupil had a bag to house the pair of shoes not being worn at the time. These bags were hung on one's peg in the cloakroom. The girls' bags were certainly red in colour. However in June 1940, with the onset of the threat of air raids, the wearing of 'house shoes' became optional and there was little reference to them, after that.

All these items were the subject of clothes rationing from July 1941 and as a result, a fair measure of 'hand-me-down' and 'make do and mend' had to be and was, carried out. A plea to old Scouts for the donation of their uniform, particularly their hats and their neckerchief, was made late in 1941. At the outset each person received 66 'clothing coupons' per year, reduced in 1943 to 40, and then up to 48 in 1944. A man's suit took 26 coupons, shirts 5, socks 3 and shoes 7. A lady's outdoor coat could take 18, blouses and jumpers 5, stockings 2, vest and knickers 3. Genuine children sizes did actually incur slightly fewer coupons than those mentioned, but overall it was a very severe imposition. I recall the observation at the time, that whereas the Scouts and Guides had to use coupons for their uniform, the ATC got theirs coupon free. Clothes rationing was finished in 1949, but during its tenure it was a serious component of schooling in the 1940s. Because of metal shortage, the boys' metal cap badge gave way to a cloth version late in 1941.

SCHOOL MOTTO, SONG AND HYMN.

As far as any records survive or memories recall, only the boys seem to have had a school motto, a school song and/or a school hymn.

The school motto was the almost hackneyed 'mens sana in corpore sano' - 'a sound mind in a healthy body'. Its only regular appearance seems to have been on the cover of the boys' school magazine and this was dropped in the early fifties, perhaps as presenting a dated image or perhaps reflecting an emerging politically correct view (as the concept became known) that it could be interpreted as discriminatory, against handicapped people.

The school song will be remembered by most boys - 'Forty years on'

Fifty years on. The Girls 1940s reunion in 1998.

Forty years on, when afar and asunder,
Parted are those who are singing today,
When you look back and forgetfully wonder,
What you were like in your work and your play-
Then it may be there will often come o'er you,
Glimpses of notes, like the catch of a song,
Visions of boyhood shall float them before you,
Echoes of dreamland shall bear them along.

Oh! The great days, in the distance enchanted,
Days of fresh air in the rain and the sun,
How we rejoiced as we struggled and panted-
Hardly believable forty years on
How we discours'd of them, one with another,
Auguring triumph, or balancing fate,
Love the ally with the heart of a brother
Hated the foe with a playing at hate

Forty years on, growing older and older,
Shorter in wind as in memory long,
Feeble of foot, and rheumatic of shoulder,
What will it help you that once you were strong?
God gives us bases to guard or beleaguer,
Games to play out, whether earnest or fun,
Fights for the fearless, and goals for the eager,
Twenty, and thirty, and forty years on.

All interspersed with the chorus,

Follow up! follow up! follow up! follow up! follow up!
Till the fields ring again and again,
With the tramp of the thirty stout men, -
Follow up! Follow up!

the penultimate 'follow up!', in each chorus, being sung by a solo treble.

It was a grand tune, full of sentiment and very easy to sing. But it had one disadvantage - it wasn't ours. It was the Harrow School song. Under what circumstance we adopted it, I have no idea but I think that it was Mr F. R. Price who eventually dropped it. However, we sang it at the first 50-year reunion in 1995, somebody having been realistic enough to bring along a soprano to sing that penultimate 'Follow up!'

The school hymn was taken from the less controversial numbers in 'Hymns - Ancient and Modern'. It was ' Where is thy God, my soul?'

However, it was not sung at the Dedication of the School War memorial in 1953, and thus neither motto, song or hymn appear to have survived beyond the 1940s, other than in peoples' recollections.

THE WAR - WORLD WAR TWO.

The all pervasive background to school life for the first half of the 'forties was, of course, World War Two. That rather chilling part of Mr. Chamberlain's address to the nation on 3rd September 1939, in which he told us '.....I have to tell you that no such undertaking has been received and consequently this country is at war with Germany.' is remembered by quite a few pupils. I think that I could tell you within a couple of square yards, where I was when I heard it.

Most things changed after that, but they in turn became the new norm. The blackout was enforced straight away. Houses could show no signs of a light within, street lights were extinguished totally, shop lighting was banned, vehicle lights were heavily shrouded, traffic lights were screened to show only a modest cross of light, after dark. A strange corollary, one might think, was that driving without lights (albeit heavily screened) was a punishable offence which was regularly enforced. Many cycles only had battery driven lights, and even when appropriate batteries were well nigh impossible to obtain, the law relating to riding without lights' was still enforced. The blackout rules were not relaxed, and then only partially, until 17th September 1944, when a modest degree of street lighting was permitted. Of course the blackout regime ensured that the classrooms could only be used during daylight hours and when Summer Time was retained into the winter months, the mornings were darker than hitherto for that time of year. School hours, already only half day at the time, had to be adjusted to cater for this new circumstance, and lessons were forced to start later. Many pupils had to set out for school in the dark.

Many will remember the 'Dig for Victory' campaign to encourage the production of home grown fruit and vegetables. Both the girls and the boys, often on a form-by-form basis had plots of land around the playing field allocated to them as allotment plots, and for a while useful crops were produced. 'Mr Middleton' was the wartime gardening expert on the BBC (sound only, of course) and 'Fud' Hill became the boys' school's 'Mr Middleton'. For the girls, Miss White performed a similar role. After the destruction of their classrooms the girls dug up their quad in furtherance of 'digging for victory'. The pupils of both schools, but particularly the girls, additionally collected rose hips (to make rose hip syrup, rich in vitamin C which helped to combat the shortages of oranges), elderberries and nettles to supplement (or support) the nation's diet. The boys' IV(i) form report in 1941 got quite excited about their new girl - Rose Hips - perhaps because time away from the classroom was allowed to gather her from bushes on Bleadon Hill. The boys harvested horse-chestnuts at one stage.

From quite early on in the war, senior boys helped the GPO with the delivery of the Christmas mail. It wasn't entirely altruistic for by the standards of the time it was quite financially rewarding. However, it could involve a regular early start and there were deliveries and thus attendance, on Sundays as well as on Christmas Day. Still it was good fun and I for one, certainly enjoyed it. Pay rates in 1945 for 'temporaries', appear to have been 1/- per hour, with time-and-a-half for Sundays and Christmas Day. Thus five hours on a Sunday morning grossed you 7/6, which would have been considered quite good.

Other aspects of the War, such as food and clothes rationing, air raids, evacuation, harvest camps, the presence of non-British, particularly US, troops, are covered elsewhere in these chapters. However, that still leaves the almost endless impact of the day's news, carried largely by the BBC and the national newspapers. The nine o'clock BBC news, was a near staple in most people's lives - there was, of course, no TV. It could carry news of victories as well as defeats and consequently it could elate or depress. For non-combatants like we pupils however, one sometimes felt unconnected with these news items, and the impact of these events on humanity was sometimes overlooked, like a disaster in a far away land even today. However, for me, British defeats at places like Crete, Tobruk, Hong Kong, Singapore somehow left a certain undefined uncertainty. Then victories, which slowly began to feature, served to improve our lot. The sinking of the 'Bismarck' cheered us up, El Alamein was sufficiently worthy for the church bells to be rung for the first time for some while, the Dambuster's raid made us feel very proud, and then D-day seemed to be the beginning of the end. As already mentioned, Roy Perry recalls that when 'Bismarck' was sunk, Mr Bateman 'romped around the school in great delight and announced that every boy to whom he had given a detention, was reprieved'. Someone has commented that a wall map with pins to show the ebb and flow of the battle lines, was itself, like a board game.

Schoolboys with an interest in anything mechanical, certainly of a military dimension, were well catered for. There was a general ebb and flow of military equipment through the town, aside from the US Army, and in the shadow factories at Banwell/Elborough and Oldmixon, we had a major aircraft manufacturing centre with test flying from Weston airport. Quite a range of aircraft based at Weston also operated in support of the air launched sea weapon trials based at HMS ' Birnbeck' - the Old Pier, which also housed the DMWD (Department for Miscellaneous Weapons Development), and was closed for the duration. The Weston aircraft factories, the aerodrome and part of the town were protected by a balloon barrage of upwards of 24 balloons. Because their role conflicted with test flying and flying training from the airport, these balloons spent much of their time close hauled, on the ground. They were only 'flown', save for practice occasions, when there was any threat of local enemy air activity, and as time went by this was mainly at night. Occasionally one would 'escape' and drag its cable across all sorts of unsuspecting territory. Some balloons were shot down during the principal raids on Weston.

It is very difficult to summarise the effect - it must have had some - that this wartime environment and all this wartime news had on our schooling. Yet, many have commented on the ordinariness of life, in those extraordinary times. This ordinariness was partly engendered by the fact there were no concessions to these distractions. School lessons were carried out with the normal amount of vigour, homework was expected to be have been done on time, exams were pursued in a non-compromising manner, and excuses were neither made nor given for the realities of those times. Behaviour and general demeanour were not compromised.

Maybe, in truth, for the majority, it was an exciting time to be growing up.

A regular feature of classroom life in the boys school was the weekly collection for the 'Red Cross and St. John Fund'. Money collected by this fund was allocated to buy parcels containing food and other necessities, for British prisoners-of -war. Each class had its collector and Mr. Pinton was the master in overall charge. By the time the school fund was wound up in June 1945, the boys' had collected £455 - a goodly sum for those days. Both schools were members of the 'Schools' National Savings Association' and National Savings stamps were purchasable at the schools. Each year during the war there was a particular national promotion of National Savings under such titles as 'Wings for Victory' week, 'Warship' week, 'Salute the Soldier' week, when most Town Halls in the land sported some sort of huge barometer reflecting that town's progress towards reaching their savings target. Weston was no exception and the boys school alone could raise (that is, to loan by way of National Savings) a figure upwards of £1500 in the week. It is just possible that some better-off parents, or teachers, were simply adjusting their portfolio, but it all sounded very impressive. On a much lower key, there were also collections for 'Aid to Russia' week and the 'Merchant Navy Comforts Fund'.

In 1942, in accordance with a Board of Education policy, the school was kept open during the summer holidays so that games or other pursuits might be organised, but the greatest number that turned up on any one day was six. There was no further mention of that policy!

The war in Europe came to an end, of course, on the 8th May 1945 (VE day). Although expected for a few days prior to that, the actual announcement was made at relatively short notice along with a declaration of two days national holiday covering the 8th and 9th May. This left no time for any celebrations at the school, although morning assemblies on the 10th May were by way of a Service of Thanksgiving. The war against Japan finished on 15th August 1945 (VJ day) when the schools were on summer holiday (or at farming camps) and the schools' celebration simply took the form of two days added on, to that holiday. There was no abrupt change to the social atmosphere or to one's normal routines, and for some, the imminent 'School Cert' or of 'Higher' examinations, loomed the larger in the way of things.

Both events, VE day and VJ day, did however see some personal jollification in Weston, and large crowds crowded the Winter Gardens, the Rozel bandstand and the sea front generally, in rather erratic dancing and untypical antics. Few of the boys had any skill in ballroom dancing, so joining a conga or the 'hokey cokey' (an activity which soon palled) was about the only composite activity that we could join in. Quite a large number of the schools' girls and boys were together on the sea front and I suspect that a certain progress was made on a broad front, in the growing up stakes. Janet Lovell (Owen) and Iris Tipple moved upmarket and went to a dance at the Melrose, on VE night. We all stayed up much later than was the norm for those times.

THE EVACUEES

Like some long-gone bomber command airfield now marked only by the sound of the breeze, it is difficult to recall that the ground cleared by the school's demolition in 1999, once echoed to the noise and happenings of four schools. These were the evacuated Barking Abbey School from Barking, Essex, the evacuated Mitcham County School from Mitcham, Surrey and the two resident Weston County schools. In fact each of the evacuated schools, were the combination of two single sex schools at their home location. It was the era of a great migration of schools from what were presumed (and often were) areas at risk from enemy bombing, to areas where that risk was presumed to be, but alas not always proved to be, minimal. It was the era of the evacuees.

Since the Munich crisis of 1938, the Government had prepared plans for a mass evacuation of children (and in the case of very young children, their mothers) away from some of the areas of mass conurbation. There had been a general presumption that heavy bombing would commence, particularly in the south east, as soon as war was declared, and the whole country was given one of three designations - evacuation, reception or neutral - with Weston, in fact Somerset overall, designated as a reception area.

In September 1939, the County School, and more particularly its double hall, became the Evacuation (Reception) Centre for the southern ward of the town. Down the main body of the hall 'row after row of chairs were set out, on which the evacuees on their arrival sat, in order to rest after their long journey while they were given light refreshment and their immediate wants attended to'. There were a host of voluntary workers, many of whom were staff or pupils at the school, assisting in this endeavour, as billeting officers, nurses, messengers, drivers and clerks etc. The school's involvement seems to be an event long since forgotten, but it is well worth recording, even if it was a few months before our decade.

Of particular interest to us is the fact that the 'evacuation area' list included the Borough of Barking, in Essex - virtually north-east London. With the rapidly deteriorating European situation towards the end of August 1939, the pupils of Barking Abbey School - their local County School - were told to be ready to be evacuated on the 28th August 1939, although in fact their evacuation was on the 1st September. The Barking Abbey party, about 250 strong, complete with luggage, gas masks and food, assembled and departed from Upney (on the District Line of the Underground) station for a destination as yet unknown. In fact they were en route to Ealing Broadway, where they transferred to a westbound steam train on the main line out of Paddington. A later recollection recalls that 'doubtless there were feelings of depression and anxiety for those left behind to face the threatened air raids and terrors', but ' later spirits rose somewhat on learning that our destination was Weston-super-Mare'. At least they must have heard of it.

Derek Porter was an evacuee from Barking, although at the time of the events recorded above he was still with his junior school - Manor School, Barking. He was evacuated on 2nd September 1939, with his mother and his young brother, then aged two, by a train which left Ilford railway station at about 7.30 in the morning and about twelve hours later arrived at the 'end of the line', as Derek describes it. To the locals it was known as Clevedon. Apparently his train should have gone to Weston where they were ready to receive young children and their mothers. The train that should have gone to Clevedon and contained older children went mistakenly to Weston. Such is (one day short of) wartime. He then passed the scholarship, which would have given him entrance to Barking Abbey School (had he still been in Barking) but family circumstances and their relocation to Weston, and the involvement of the Somerset Education Committee found him as a pupil at Weston County School. There, contemporaries will know, he finished up as Head Boy, and is of course the author of much of the 'Boys Staff' section of these recollections.

The whole story of Barking Abbey's reception as evacuees is beyond the scope and remit of this recollection, but contemporary and later accounts all praise the organisation that confronted them on arrival - it was about 9.00 pm, wet and dark, and they must have all been very tired. Of the people involved with their reception, one Barking Abbey account recalls that 'they were untiring in their efforts to get the pupils placed in homes where they felt they were wanted'. By some quirk, Barking Abbey weren't processed through the County School reception centre, but through centres at Grove Park and Locking Road school, and as a result they tended to finish up billeted in the northern end of the town. The 16th September 1939 edition of 'The Weston Mercury' carried a letter from the Barking Abbey head master - Col E. A. Loftus - in which he was generous in his praise for the 'kindly hospitality accorded to them at this beautiful resort by the sea'. However he went on, 'perhaps I might suggest that the troops in the vicinity may extend a similar chivalry towards the evacuated schoolgirls by not accosting them in the streets'. To this day, some of the girls recall this as a bit of a hoot, but apparently the Colonel was held in high esteem by his pupils and sadly missed when he died at the age of 103.

The next priority was schooling - Weston County School was to provide the accommodation.

At the outset, Barking Abbey (Mitcham had not yet arrived) shared both the Boys County school and the Girls County school. Barking had the premises between 1.30pm. and 5.30pm, Monday to Friday, and between 9.00 and 12.30 on Saturdays. Our own County School had the premises in the weekday mornings - originally, 7.50 am to 12.50pm, but this had to be modified to 8.35 am to 1.10 pm in the 1940 winter, because Summer Time had been retained and it was still dark at 7.50 am. Additionally Weston Boys (at least) decided to reverse the order of lessons every three weeks in order to lessen the effect of the inevitable late arrivals to school. Weston arranged their sporting activities for the afternoon. For Barking, sporting activities took place in the mornings, whilst additional lessons were occasionally also held in the morning in vacant rooms or elsewhere in the town. Influenced additionally by longer terms and shorter holidays, hours under tuition were actually greater than the peacetime norm. Nevertheless with the initial absence of the perceived threat, there was a slow migration back to Barking and numbers began to dwindle. One account mentions 278 down to 180.

Oversexed and over here?   Mitcham County pupils with Weston friends. School caps had to be worn at all times.

Although Barking Abbey had largely separated boys and girls schools at home it does not appear to have been enforced with quite the vigour that was the norm at Weston. In their evacuated circumstance they were a wholly mixed school. This bought joy to the hearts (at least) of Weston girls. June Hale recalls that "When I first started at the school there was strictly no real contact with the boys school next door - we were in real trouble if we talked to them in uniform at all. Then came our evacuees, Mitcham County School next door and Barking Abbey to us, a mixed school! We had social events together occasionally and we were very curious to find out who sat in our desks when we weren't there. Some of us had boys, so we wrote notes and, of course were found out and 'up before Miss Farthing'...." Barking celebrated Christmas with parties for juniors and seniors, and a 'dance for the combined sixth forms and staff from the (eventual) four schools'. There must have been some in the Weston firmament who thought that this would surely lead to licentious behaviour and risking results that could be barely contemplated. I was not involved in any such school sponsored mixing in the whole of the subsequent years of the decade.

Mitcham County School came to Weston on 3rd October 1940. This was as the night blitz on London got under way and Mitcham was included in the evacuation scheme for the first time. Like those before us, for I was one of them, we had no idea of where we were going. We were put on buses at the school, found ourselves at Paddington station and then put on a train. It was not until the following morning in a house on Beach Road (via a Reception Centre at Locking Road school) that I found out where we were - not that Weston-super-Mare meant much to me at the time. It was the era when all road and railway signs had been removed and the Locking Road excursion platform where we arrived had given us no clue. In fact I had travelled with an elementary school that I had only joined that very morning. There were two of us lone travellers, and other than each other we did not know another soul, neither pupils or teachers. It was not until December 1940 that I joined Mitcham County for the first time - at Broadoak Road.

Those who travelled with their normal school and thus with teachers and pupils that they knew, had perhaps a marginally, but only marginally, easier time. Mrs Pamela Starling from Mitcham has sent me copies of letters that she wrote to a friend (who had fortunately kept them and had returned them in recent months) just after she arrived at Weston and which told of her first impressions of the County School. Originally, along with many of her school (Mitcham County School for Girls) she was originally billeted at 'Highbury', otherwise the Methodist Holiday Home, in Atlantic Road. She was then moved to Slimeridge Farm in Uphill with two others and the sheer joy of that life and the welcome they received from the owners, Mr. and Mrs. Bowley, is manifest in her letters, and a joy to read. Additionally, she has written,

> ' We go to the Weston County School. It is a beautiful school. We are in the boys' wing because we are sharing it with Mitcham County Boys. It is awfully funny with them. Some say such silly things in the lessons that it makes you laugh. We have masters most of the time. We have not had any of our mistresses yet but I expect we will. The masters are very strict. Some of them are horrible and grumpy, but some are awfully pleasant. The school is built in a awfully healthy fashion All the walls are built of glass and it all opens out. The roof is built of brick and concrete. ...there is a marvellous gym here When it is sunny we have all the glass doors open. Its lovely.'

All familiar stuff of course to the residents but a very good overview from one who had only just arrived under fairly traumatic circumstances. Seemingly school mistresses weren't necessarily paragons of friendliness. The girls billeted at 'Highbury' were in the care of their French, French mistress. Mrs Starling relates in one of her letters, 'she was terrible. She made a lot of rules of her own. We were not allowed out after tea, not allowed to eat sweets or ices in the street, not allowed to take our hats off, not allowed to speak to boys, not allowed to walk on wet sands - she was a goof'. The underlying message seems vaguely familiar.

So the Weston school buildings now had to accommodate yet another school. This was effected by Barking Abbey sharing only the Girls' school and Mitcham County School sharing the Boys', more or less on the same time divide as with just the one evacuated school. The same morning and afternoon split with the local residents prevailed, but space pressures were mounting. By this time the school was at full stretch and some relief was found by hiring the Moorland Road Congregational hall more or less full time. This was shared by the schools on a basis similar to the sharing of the main building. Again Mitcham Boys and Mitcham Girls were separate in Mitcham but coeducational at Weston. Early on in the war a lady wrote to the 'Weston Mercury' as a mother who had her own children and also fostered evacuees. With the changeover at lunch time, this complicated her arrangements for what was probably the principle meal of the day - her own children needing a late lunch, her evacuees needing an early one. She thought that the authorities should reconsider their original plans and have the two groups go to *full day* schooling on *alternate* days. Perhaps not unexpectedly, this nice bit of lateral thinking didn't find sympathy with the powers that be, and it was never implemented.

Until late June 1942 (when the girls' school was burned down, and Barking lost all their school records) this arrangement for the four schools assumed a certain normality. There were inter-school (single sex) matches between all the schools in nearly all the sports practised at the time, and there was support and co-operation between the ATC squadrons and the Scouts of the schools.

However, as related later in the 'After the Air Raid' chapter, both Barking and Mitcham had to forgo any sharing of the surviving school buildings after that air raid and they returned to London in July 1942. During the V1 and V2 attacks on the south-east, in 1944, Weston was again earmarked as a reception area - I still have my Scout roll-up list, so that we might be called up to help at short notice - but the need was never invoked.

Barking Abbey still have an active group (The Barkabbeyans) who have been very helpful with these recollections. The Mitcham County Schools, alas, almost appeared to have disappeared off the face of the

earth, until Mrs Starling (above) replied to a letter that I had written to a local Mitcham paper.

AIR RAIDS.

From June 1940 to March 1944 Weston, its population, and hence pupils at the school were party to both the threats and the realities of air raids of varying severity, the majority of them at night. In most cases, the air raid warnings that were experienced reflected raids on Bristol and Cardiff or for raiders bound for further north. In most cases, but with notable exceptions, there appeared no immediate local threat. Residents thus slept reasonably soundly in their own beds even though the sirens had sounded, and the noise of gunfire and the drone of aircraft engines would have been commonplace. School on the following day, in turn, reflected a certain normality for there would have been no concessions for disturbed sleep. If the threat appeared more substantial resort could be made in many homes (in later months) to the Morrison indoor steel shelter, to surface shelters in the streets or just as commonly, to 'under the stairs'. Alison Day learned to play many card games, including bezique and solo whist whilst under the stairs' and later like many others, played table tennis on top of her Morrison shelter. One wonders

A Morrison table shelter

if the modern game of table tennis might not be enlivened by a few bolt heads protruding above the playing surface - the standard hazard with the Morrison shelter as a table tennis table.

The only likely official role in the Civil Defence forces that school pupils were likely to play, were as messengers with the ARP (Air Raid Precaution) or AFS (Auxiliary Fire Service)- a job that was not without its hazard. Originally, various youth services were the source of these messengers, particularly the Scouts, and John Owen's experience is related later in this chapter. However the government became concerned that there might be casualties among very young people and thus formalised the Messenger service into the Civil Defence structure with a minimum age of 16 - maybe 15. In such circumstance the participants had a uniform and were given an official tin hat. One school form report commented that the tin hats of two of its members hanging on hooks at the back of the class 'gave us a feeling of confidence and security'. Later, senior boys were enrolled as 'firewatchers' for duty at the school, and for two of them this proved a very vulnerable job indeed, as we shall see. These firewatchers were paid 1/6d (7.5p) per night, given a stirrup pump, but no tin hat. Presumably, they were not 'official', although following the heavy fire-bomb raids elsewhere in 1941, the government required all properties to have some measure of firewatch duty on the premises.

In June 1940, the deteriorating war situation with the fall of France was beginning to have its effects on the school. Emergency air raid positions were allocated within the school and macintoshes as well as gas masks were bought into the classrooms. Barriers were erected by the school on the playing field 'to prevent hostile landings from the air'. Bryan Jones remembers that, even before he joined the school somehow he went by coach with 'Air Cadets under the control of 'Curly' Hay' to build piles of stones on the Mendips to thwart glider landings'. He cannot recall how he got involved; he was only 11 at the time. Examinations, and lessons in general, were beginning to be interrupted by air raid warnings. The frequency of these interruptions were such that having taken due advice, the school eventually decided to carry on normally at the outset of an alert, until an appointed spotter detected more immediate danger and sounded an internal alarm. In fact such an event never arose. A Barking Abbey recollection recalls that whilst they were at Weston (1939-1942) the siren sounded over 500 times and they, like Weston County, resorted to a 'spotter', to limit the disruption to lessons.

The first, and probably the only, substantial daylight activity which, superficially at least, seemed to be a threat was on 25th September 1940. On that day 58 Heinkel 111's escorted by 52 Messerschmitt 110's were routed for a raid on The Bristol Aeroplane Co. at Filton. Approaching the Dorset coast around Portland, the British assessment of the raid was that the Westland works at Yeovil was the target. Our fighters were vectored accordingly. Until this mistake was appreciated this large formation of enemy aircraft flew 'serenely and unmolested' over the Somerset levels, towards Weston where they turned over the Channel for their run in to Filton. This sudden appearance of such a large formation in a clear September sky caused some consternation at the school. Some classes seemed to have been rushed into the cloakroom, where they sat under their appropriate coat peg, some were directed to the hall where they were told to sit around the walls, some girls had to lie on the gym floor, whilst other pupils got to the trenches that had been dug along the edge of the playing field - all probably part of the prearranged plan. Those who were outdoors saw what was, by all accounts, a very impressive formation 'with their black crosses clearly visible'. Don Andrews however recalls that 'an indulgent master who allowed us to go into the quad and look up into the bright blue sky', but 'no-one could recognise the types of planes as they flew high above'.

There was, of course, no damage to the school or to anywhere near. However, the damage to Filton was substantial and serious and the casualties were very high. From the German point of view it was a very successful raid.

A number of people recall these trenches which were just inside the fence on the far side of the playing field. Prior to these trenches, Barking Abbey pupils were instructed to run out on to the playing field and lie flat, but getting them then all back into class on the sounding of the all-clear proved troublesome. The trenches were then dug. At the outset they were dug, cleaned and maintained on a form-by-form basis and there seemed some resentment in one form when they, who had shown pride in their bit of real estate had to hand it over to another form who had not shown such commitment. They were even more displeased when it was announced that the trenches would not be used in the event of an air raid, in any case. However, both Barking Abbey and Weston pupils recall the trenches' propensity of filling with water (at high tide?), and thus were abandoned after a very short period. Howard Ellis of Barking Abbey relates, 'improved instructions were [then] rapidly issued - we were to sally forth from the School and run to the woods nearby into which we were to scatter - boys on one side of the road, girls on the other. ' School proprieties had to be observed'. However a better scheme was obviously needed and a survey was made of supposedly safe places within the school building, he concludes. Mary Thomas also remembers 'trooping across the playing field when the siren went, making our way to Uphill Manor'.

Trevor Rowsell remembers that the trenches were dug in a zig-zag format and during early practices, pupils would lob lumps of mud from one zig to the next zag onto their colleagues, as simulated hand grenades. Teachers apparently looked displeased at these mud splattered returnees to the classroom.

On the night of 3rd/4th September 1940, Banwell was extremely unfortunate when it was hit by a stick of bombs dropped at random by a German bomber. The bombs seemed to straddle the main road through the village and five people were killed, including the father of a pupil at the Girls' School.

Weston suffered its first serious air raid in the late evening and early hours of Saturday/Sunday, 4th/5th January 1941. A raid destined for Avonmouth Docks drifted down the coast, as the primary target became obscured by cloud. Weston was clear and although not the initial target, a sharp attack took place upon it, with 34 killed and 85 injured. There

Bomb damage at Banwell in September 1940

was no damage to the school but Peter Weaver who was yet to join the school was fortunate that his father had built a strong air raid shelter in the basement of their house in Mendip Road. A bomb dropped almost opposite his house causing a fatality, but his own family and neighbours sharing the shelter were unharmed. The front of his house had been blown in and he remembers that 'all the roof tiles that had been lifted by the blast were piled neatly along the guttering edge'. In the school magazine later that year, there was an article written by a fifth former, G. Webb, entitled 'An untoward event'. It describes being trapped in their pantry where they had taken shelter, after bombs had fallen in close proximity. It relates how 'all was quiet except for the pitter patter of grit and small pieces of plaster that fell in our ears, noses and mouths nearly choking us and giving us sore throats for days to come - days that at that moment we thought that we would never live to see'. They were eventually rescued but seven houses had been completely demolished.

Overall, the raid was a significant and quite frightening occasion and a possible repeat was a component to the background of schooling in those days.

Bristol remained a major target (and thus a continuing threat to Weston residents) for the German Luftwaffe. These heavy night raids on Bristol, culminated with the Good Friday raid on 11th April 1941. On the previous Friday, a Heinkel 111 was shot down by a Bristol 'Beaufighter', perhaps made at Weston, operating from Middle Wallop, and it crashed at Hewish. The school seems to have been well represented among those who went to have a look. Two of the German crew who were killed are buried in Weston cemetery, the other three, including the pilot, became Prisoners of War.

As far as the school was concerned everything came to a head on the weekend of 27th/28th June 1942. For the first time, Weston was the defined target. Two raids, each by about 50 bombers, on successive nights targeted the town with incendiaries and high explosives, in the clear light of a full moon.

Although the raids took place during the tenure of the German Baedeker series of retaliatory raids, many post-war observers do not think that it is correctly included in that programme. Weston was probably a legitimate target, by the standards of those days.

On the second of the two nights, that is the night of 28th/29th June 1942, two prefects, (Brian Baiden and Frank Ashby) reported for duty at the School at about 7.30 pm.

Well, let Frank Ashby tell the story....

"On June 28th, Brian Baiden and I checked in about 7.30 pm and settled into our heady surroundings [the staff room], and try to complete that day's scholastic challenges.

Accompanying us on this occasion, as usual, was a master, this time a relative newcomer to the staff, who seemed not to relish his assignment. The evening hours of daylight passed uneventfully, and although the air raid sirens were soon to sound, this was quite normal. It was not until after dark that the fun started. The unusual noise of aircraft and the ack-ack guns firing in the distance suggested that something unusual was afoot.

Our noble guardian for the night insisted that we abandon quarters and take shelter in a kind of janitors closet near the boys' locker room. As the noise grew louder and we could smell smoke, Brian and I refused to stay in this dungeon and, kid like, wanted to see what was going on, this despite the protests of our superior, who apparently feared imminent destruction, and remained secluded therein.

As Brian and I emerged into the central quad, I remember letting out a whoop of glee, thinking that one of the planes had been bought down in a massive ball of fire, only to discover that it was just a barrage balloon bought down towards Hutton, no doubt by 'friendly fire'.[In fact there is a fair amount of evidence that the German aircraft in their low level attacks did shoot at the barrage balloons]

Meanwhile a small number of incendiary bombs had come down in the quad, luckily avoiding the surrounding roofs, with the exception of the woodwork shop in the northeast corner, next to the staff room. Not knowing what the results of our action might be we blithely got hold of sandbags which lay here and there in the cloistered corridors, and used them to quell the canisters which seemed like potent fireworks. The incendiaries in the woodwork shop were difficult to get at because the door was firmly locked, its upper half of glass being covered with mesh.

We then remembered that on a wall in the school secretary's office (by name, Ruth), there was a hatchet, and so we made for that and proceeded to hack away the glass and mesh, and climbed through into the shop. We hauled in sand bags and managed to quell the beginning fires and stifle the incendiaries.

As the boys half of the school seemed now secure, Brian and I made for the girls' section which was by then almost fully engulfed having been struck by a very considerable number of these fire bombs. At this time I was working for a Higher School Certificate in History, French and English (Brian was taking Science subjects), along with E.J. Harriss, known as Ticker, whose father ran a clock shop in Orchard Street. E. J. and I had a number of lady teachers from the girls' staff for our courses, among whom was a certain Miss Campbell, a formidable individual, whose special interest was the French Revolution (and boy did we have a dose of that period). Any way, her classroom was one of the few whose roof had not collapsed and I suppose feeling like a knight in shining armour, I managed to rescue the said Campbell's books and gown and other items before that classroom roof also caved in.

By that time a fire brigade unit had arrived and was able to prevent the fire spreading to the area under the central clock tower and the auditorium nearby. There was nothing more Brian and I could do, so we climbed on our bikes and headed for home along Beach Road littered with fire hoses.

June Hale found her very singed Report Book on the grass outside her burnt-out form room. Miss Campbell was her form mistress. It is possible that this is one of the books rescued by Frank Ashby.

In the course of the night my parents had been told that the school had been destroyed (which for them was the cause of some alarm) and so they set off around 5 a.m. in pyjamas and dressing gowns trying to discover whether their offspring was secure. Brian and I met them by chance near the Sanatorium and much to their relief, we headed home for breakfast.

Then it was back to school for the opening as usual.

It was the custom at the time for two prefects to be stationed at the access door of the school on Broadoak Road, to keep an eye on youngsters coming in, making sure that ties were straight and that red and yellow caps were in place. That same morning after the fires, Brian and I were, by chance, on duty and so there we were, wearing gauntlets which covered only very superficial burns and scratches.

Strangely enough I cannot remember any school official expressing thanks for our efforts, although I'm sure that some of the staff must have done so. The kids of course said,' Why didn't you let it burn?'.

So thats the story of this incident, tiny in the scheme of things but I think it was the excitement of the night which had the greatest impression upon us".

It is worth recalling that these incendiary bombs were quite threatening. They were typically 1kg in weight, about 2" in diameter and about 18"

Bomb damage, probably in Malvern Road.

long, including the tail. They had a thermite filling which ignited the magnesium casing. By 1942 a number of these bombs were made harder and much more dangerous to combat, by the addition of a small explosive charge in the nose or in the tail. They could be dropped in clusters of several hundred.

Other pupils also had very frightening moments. Janet Lovell (Williams), whose father owned the chemists at the south end of St. James Street, recalls that when a stick of incendiary bombs fell on that street 'we nearly lost our lives from smoke inhalation'. Janet's family crawled along their hall on their hand and knees with wet handkerchiefs over their noses. Her father carried his briefcase, her mother her handbag, her young brother his teddy, and Janet carried Panda the

family cat. When they got out into the street they were 'rained on by burning splinters'. From there, they were evacuated to relatives near Crook Peak. Janet became Head Girl in 1949. In fact their premises survived the raid but not so the properties just behind them.

Derek Porter lived in that part of Locking Road which backed on to the sidings that were part of Weston railway station. On the first night, a bomb nearly demolished a nearby signal box breaking every window and removing half the slates off the Porter home. On the second night, incendiaries seemed to pose the main threat. One hit the household shed and Derek was called on by his father to help with the stirrup pump, to put out the flames. But just over their garden fence Derek describes ' the awesome sight' of two long lines of railway carriages on fire, from end to end.

Margaret England, who lived in Malvern Road also had a lucky escape. People living opposite them were killed and her own house was badly damaged. Margaret remembers that the blast caused all the cupboard doors of her home to open, sucking out all the crockery. The ceilings then came down breaking 'most of our pretty cups and saucers' which in the short term could only be replaced by plain white crockery. Her family had to stay with friends at Milton whilst necessary repairs were done to the roof and 'the windows were boarded up to deter looters'.

The following days must have been utterly confusing. However, as Frank Ashby records, pupils turned up on the Monday morning and were expected to be properly attired. It is this near normality which seems so remarkable. The boys' lessons seemed to recommence forthwith. Of course, many girls and boys turned up at school, not without considerable difficulty, quite unaware of the damage to the school. June and Marian Hale whose journey from home involved two buses recalls the diversions that those buses had to take, first to get into town (the 154) and then from the town to Broadoak Road (the 90). The 90 route was particularly affected. They were quite unaware 'that the school had been incinerated'. They remember the smell of sulphur (more likely, magnesium) and the bits of incendiary cases over the playing fields. Because of damage to Weston station and to the track, train pupils from Yatton had to transfer to buses somewhere along the route. The bus alternative took them to Broadoak Road and as it turned the corner Gus Fletcher recalls that there was a spontaneous cheer from girls and boys alike, at the sight of the smoking ruins.

The girls, at least those who were not taking state examinations, were not surprisingly given a week off, although Janet Lovell (Owen) who had joined the school mid-term, recalls that one of her first memories of the school is of hunting through 'the burnt out rubble where my classroom had been' and finding her prayer book. Mitcham certainly restarted normal lessons that afternoon. I remember attending.

Janet Lovell's future husband - John 'Coronation' Owen - watched the raid from the roof of the family home - the 'Coronation Hotel', and then when it was over, went in Scout uniform to the Town Hall as a Boy Scout messenger. He apparently *did*

Pat Eagles sits on some recovered stonework from the damaged school.

have a tin helmet. He was collared by a couple of Bomb Recognition Officers whose job was to identify unexploded bombs - being a Scout there was a general presumption that he would know his way about the town. At one point he misheard them and went to the wrong road. They eventually arrived at the right spot up near Worlebury golf course, only moments after the bomb had gone off 'with a big bang'.

I, also, remember reporting to the Town Hall the following morning, as a would be messenger although at that time I was not a Scout. Somehow or other I had acquired a Home Guard tin hat. I think I might have got involved with a sort of missing persons enquiry service, but after a couple of what seemed desultory assignments it all went quiet and I went back to school that afternoon - rather fancifully perhaps, in that tin hat.

Some of the girls were allowed to help the WVS with the trucks taking tea and sandwiches to workers who were searching and clearing the bomb rubble. They went through the road barriers 'feeling very much part of the scene', as one has recorded.

Later in 1942 one pupil of the school, John Miles, who was 13 at the time, was officially commended in the London Gazette for 'meritorious service during the air raid on Weston-super-Mare". He had assisted quite bravely with fire fighting in the Trewartha Park district during the course of the raid, but the school magazine only formally announced this Commendation and made no reference to its circumstance.

However with the destruction of the Girls' classrooms, there simply was no chance of continuing to house the four schools on the site, and as a result Barking went back to Barking, and Mitcham went back to Mitcham. The threat to London at that time appeared to have diminished.

After that, the air raid threat although always potentially potent somewhat faded away. There were occasional incidents through 1943 but the final incidents in Weston were on the 27th March 1944, when a large number of phosphorous incendiary bombs fell on the Bourneville estate but caused minimal damage. Kenneth Tucker, newly arrived in Weston recalls that 'we dutifully trooped across to a brick shelter at the foot of Devonshire Road bridge when the sirens sounded only to be told shortly afterwards to get out as quickly as possible. An unexploded bomb had fallen right outside the doorway'. My own diary entry for that night reads rather laconically 'Air raid at night. IB's [incendiary bombs] dropped on Milton. Not much HE. [high explosive]'. Sadly among those relatively few high explosive bombs was one that destroyed a bungalow in Hutton, killing four people and injuring a further three. I remember going to have a look at a burnt out bungalow just off Milton Road, in the early hours, after the raid was over. Many people seem to remember the Devonshire Road UXB (unexploded bomb) because it disrupted those who journeyed to the school, along Drove/Devonshire Roads. They had to carry their cycles over the adjoining footbridge. Polly Price seems to recall that a gang of Italian prisoners of war turned up to find the bomb, but they never did so. Presumably it is no longer there?

The final threat to the Bristol area came on 15th May 1944, after which the Luftwaffe's diminished resources were concentrated on the invasion ports along the south coast. The area might have been victim of the V1 pilotless missiles, for launch ramps were built on the Cherbourg peninsular for an onslaught on to the Bristol area, but the launch area was overrun by American forces in June 1944, before the missiles could be deployed.

It was all over.

THE AFTERMATH OF THE 1942 AIR RAID.

The destruction of much of the girls' school inevitably made a big impact on the whole school regime. All ten classrooms of the girls' school were destroyed along with the chemistry lab, the physics lab and the rooms equipped for domestic science. The area that housed the teaching staff and the Head Mistress also disappeared. There is some recollection that the blaze really got underway in this laboratory/administrative area and then swept through the roofing voids which connected all the classrooms. Thus this whole area, virtually the whole girls' school, became uninhabitable. On the day following the raids, Barking Abbey (and Mitcham) pupils had to sit the Higher School Certificate and the General School Examination papers. Weston pupils were working under the auspices of another authority. Barking Abbey's papers however had been burned in the conflagration and so they had to 'borrow' the papers from Mitcham after the Mitcham pupils had finished with them. There was no instant photocopying, in those days. Barking Abbey took their 'morning' exams, between 12 p.m. and 3 p.m. and the 'afternoon' papers between

Mitcham County School
at Weston- Super- Mare
Seventh July 1942

Dear Parent,
          After the recent air raids on Weston-super-Mare there have had to be alterations in the arrangements for this school.
          Owing to the damage done to the school here, the Somerset Education Committee feel that they can no longer offer us the use of buildings in Weston which we have so far enjoyed.
          The decision for each child must be left in the parents hands.
          Should you decide to leave him or her in Weston, arrangements will be made for continued secondary education at one of the local county schools.
          Should you wish for reevacuation to another reception area, it can be arranged and suitable provision will be made in the new area for continued education.
          Should you decide to have your child back in Mitcham the Boys and Girls County Schools will be open for instruction at all stages of school life,including the sixth form. I think it likely that all members of the present staff here will be available for service in Mitcham next term.
          The school here will close for instruction on or about 24th July. The school in Mitcham will reopen 15th September, there is no reason why those whose parents decide to have them back in Mitcham should return immediately term breaks up.,they are entitled to remain evacuated until their return is arranged.
          The Air Training Corps camp will take place as arranged from 17th to 24th August at Halton.
          We were grateful that there was no injury to a child of this school , and I know that parents will be glad to know that their behaviour both during and after the raid has been excellent.
          London University are fully aware of the effect that the raids may have had on examination candidates and will make all allowances possible.
          I should be glad if you would write to me and give me your decision as soon as possible so that I may make the necessary plans.
          In particular I hope that those parents who had been thinking of sixth form work for their boy or girl will not allow these changes to affect the decision adversely.

          yours sincerely,

The letter sent by the Mitcham headmaster to all parents, after the air raid.

5 p.m.and 8 p.m. By the following day the Mitcham papers had been duplicated for the Barking pupils and by Wednesday a new set of papers had arrived for Barking. On the Friday previous to the raid some of the Weston girls had been taking their Oxford School Certificate in Domestic Science but the results were largely lost in the conflagration. Later on, when they continued with their written examinations a contemporary remembers that they felt 'that they were now part of the war effort'.

On 15th July 1942, pupils at the school were told to gather at the end of the school drive, along Windwhistle Lane, to wave at a motorcade. They came away in the belief that it was King George VI, but in fact it was the Duke of Kent, who had come to pay his own personal tribute to the people of Weston.

The first long term impact was that Mitcham County and Barking Abbey went back to London. In the words of the letter that the Mitcham head sent to all Mitcham parents, 'The Somerset Education Committee feel that they can no longer offer us the use of the buildings in Weston which we have so far enjoyed' - somewhat of an understatement. In the case of Barking Abbey, of course, the buildings that they had 'enjoyed' weren't even there.

This left the County School girls and the County School boys, to share the surviving accommodation, which was mainly the boys' school. The ten boys' classrooms were shared half each - or was it six-four? - girls taking the south side and the boys, the north. John Owen's hope that the boys and the girls would be *sharing* classes was dashed from the outset. Prior to this, moving from the north side to the south side had been taken by some boys as evidence of achieving the status of 'full blown seniors'. Alas this pleasure was now denied them. The boys' five classrooms on the north side were largely allocated as a permanent home for one of the third forms and for the two fourth forms and the two fifth forms. This spanned my era so my contemporaries were never seriously inconvenienced. The various laboratories and the art rooms were forced into use as classrooms whilst the girls geography room, the medical room and sundry other spaces, such as the hall, the gym and the cloakrooms all became makeshift classrooms. The girls also had lessons in the Wyndham Hall in Sunnyside Road. It was the younger pupils who bore the brunt of the disruption. It must have been a nightmare for the staff to organise. There were joint lessons for the girls and boys who were taking 'arts' in the sixth form, but the girls and boys taking sixth form 'science' only shared lessons in Chemistry. Alison Day recalls that the three girls would sit

Girls sunning themselves in the dishevelled quad with the damaged west end of the school in the background. The greenhouse seems to have survived

together slightly separated from the boys but 'we paired up with the boys for practicals'. *Now* she tells us. However, against all these difficulties there was clearly a decision to provide full day schooling for both schools, and this spanned the hours of 0845 to 1250 in the morning and 1420 to 1550, in the afternoon.

The girls' staff had lost their staff room and they were housed in a very poor environment in what had been the crush hall for the girls end of the school hall. They probably had the hardest task of all. Miss Farthing found accommodation in the rooms housing the boys' headmaster. There was a doubling up even within each school. Alison Day remembers as a sixth former working at the back of a fifth form class whilst she was involved in the task of chloroforming cockroaches, presumably for dissection. One escaped from her chloroformed pad and her ensuing scream must have been quite a distraction for the fifth

formers. She additionally remembers the smell of formalin as they worked on the dissection of a dogfish and later, a frog.

Alas, the boys had no 'domestic science' facilities to share. To address this problem the girls had to go to Locking Road Senior Girls' school, a journey approaching 2 miles. They had to make their own way there. Marian Hale recalls that they went to Locking Road, one afternoon a week, and alternated between cooking one week and sewing the next. Marian goes on 'I cannot really remember sewing any garment, but I must have learned something, for today I can produce quite a respectable hem, back and herring bone stitch. The cooking almost put me off for life. For a start it was a headache for our mothers to produce the prescribed ingredients because of rationing and general food shortages. The main drawback for me was the lack of time to finish anything. By the time that one got there and got organised it was time to go home. I distinctly remember walking home with half-finished tomato soup, although, luckily I lived fairly near to Locking Road School'. When the time came to choose one's subject options in the third form, as the girls did, Marian decided to do Art and not Domestic science (you couldn't do both) arguing that one could always learn to cook later in life. In fact the Locking Road situation was not new for it had been used by the girls school in the era of half day schooling.

About one year after the raid, the local press announced that the Somerset Education Committee was prepared to consider proposals for the rebuilding of three classrooms 'subject to the omissions of ceilings and heating system and to the total cost of the work not exceeding £500'. It was not clear if ceilings and heating would come from another budget, or whether such flipperies were deemed to be unnecessary luxuries in wartime. A further year later however, in May 1944, the school magazine reported that ' the three classrooms have now been rebuilt but it has so far proved impossible to obtain desks and chairs to furnish them'. Nevertheless, by 1947 only two of the boys' classrooms were still being occupied by the girls and the rebuilding of all the classrooms, plus some prefabricated constructions, were complete by 1950. Thus for the first time for seven years, the boys had their full

Judy Price faces the reality of getting her soup back to Yatton

complement of rooms and the use of Moorland Road church hall was relinquished. The girls were back on their home territory. The roofing of the reconstruction was, however, of corrugated sheeting, not the original tiles, and this among other things, always made this rebuilt part of the school look rather 'kutcha'. But segregation had been re-established.

One adaptation, but not until 1947, was turning the ATC hut on the playing field into a home, or a classroom for the boys' sixth form. We cleared it out on the 8th and 9th September 1947 and 'moved in' on the following day. (My diary survives). It had a coke stove at its centre (it was, after all, only like a large garage) which was hardly adequate to heat it, although there was a short lived attempt to warm our morning-break milk on it. I cannot remember if we used a saucepan or had enamelled mugs. There were no facilities for washing anything up - indeed there were no facilities, period. I do not remember us staying there for long. It wasn't very practical. However it was used again in September 1949, when the number of boys returning to the fifth form created the need for a third fifth form. It was they who were accommodated 'without much comfort' in the ATC hut.

The sixth form of both schools, each of about 20 in number, were scattered all over the place, even during the ATC hut era. In truth though, this was nothing new. There seemed to have been no provision for housing a sixth form in the original school plans. They never had had

a permanent home and a presumption of small numbers had seemed to permit an assumption that the occasional empty classroom would meet their needs. Indeed, in the post-raid period classrooms were normally found for 6th form lessons, but any space not big enough to be used as classroom, such as broom cupboards, store rooms, vestibules, even the clock tower, became home to small knots of sixth formers for private study and for places where they might store their books. Although sixth form work did not involve full time teaching, full-day attendance was always mandatory, and thus everyone had to find a reasonably permanent hidey-hole. All this became the norm, it was commonplace, and most of those who recall it later in life seem to remember the whole era more in terms of the forced erosion of the segregation policy - when the rigid east-west divide had perforce to give way to a more fragile north-south divide - than in terms of any hardship or disadvantage.

It was a way of life that continued until near the end of the decade.

AMERICAN FORCES IN WESTON

In October 1943, American troops started to arrive in the town. At one level, because of their numbers, they were all pervasive, at another level they were just another group of transient military personnel that passed through the town. They were in Weston in quite large numbers until just prior to D-day on 6th June 1944. Even for us as schoolchildren however, they bought a new dimension to our awareness of the world, with their general generosity, smart uniforms, their cigarettes packed in a different way to the British norm, and the seemingly endless supplies of chewing gum. As related earlier, Miss Farthing feared the temptations or opportunities that they presented her girls, whilst for many boys their army equipment which they were often happy to show you, was a source of much interest. There is no doubt that whilst they were with us, they skewed much of our awareness of the war, in their direction. For many residents, it was their first sighting of black people, and Worle received national publicity when the vicar's wife expressed some very reactionary attitudes on how blacks should be treated ('serve them but tell them not to come back'). Black soldiers were vigorously segregated from white troops in the US Army, at that time.

The majority of the American forces in Weston seemed to be associated with anti-aircraft battalions - or what they called and still call, 'triple-A' (AAA), anti-aircraft artillery. Much of the Beach Lawns, the approach road to the Old Pier, a large area near the water tower in Weston woods and Weston golf links, hosted their guns. Only in the woods, and perhaps on the golf links, were the guns in emplacements (gun pits), evidence of which, in the woods, survives to this day. Elsewhere the

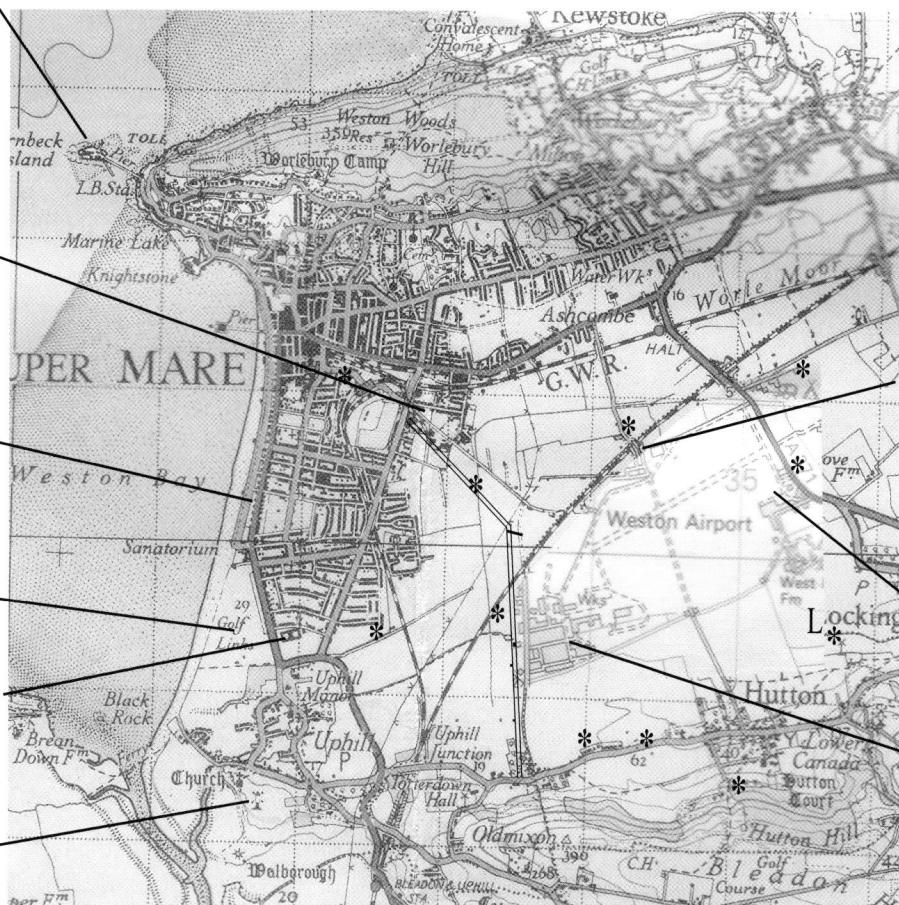

HMS 'Birnbeck' (Old Pier)
Miscellaneous Weapons
Development (DMWD)

From Yatton,
Clevedon etc

Weston Gas Works
Manufacture of
Hydrogen gas

US Army anti-aircraft
Battalions (1943/44 only)

Flight Shed. Final
Assembly of Bristol
Beauforts made at Elborough

From Banwell,
Blagdon etc.

Heavy anti-aircraft
Gun Site

Weston Airport
General aircraft
maintenance

County School

Oldmixon Aircraft
Factory - manufacture
of Bristol Beaufighters.

Observer Corps post

From Highbridge
and Burnham

* barrage balloon sites
(approximate positions
only)

Reproduced by kind permission of Ordnance Survey
© Crown Copyright NC/2005/44695

The map is divided
into 1kM squares

The proximity of the County School to wartime defence and manufacturing sites.

guns were in almost display array. This was particularly true on the Beach Lawns where a number of 'Automatic Weapons Battalions' set up their guns. These comprised mainly M55 quad mounted .50 calibre machine guns on half-track vehicles and 40mm. Bofors guns. The Beach Lawns seemed to be full of them. I don't think that they ever fired whilst they were there. On the Old Pier approach road, up in the woods and on the golf links they had Gun Battalions equipped with 90mm (static) anti-aircraft guns. There were also other units of the US Army, in Weston. Gerald Martin had two members of the 101st Airborne Division billeted on his family, for instance, and Bryan Jones' family hosted four officers who landed on Omaha beach early on D-Day.

The presence of the US Army had a number of subtle and not so subtle effects on our schooling. The more wayward (or imaginative) of our colleagues seemed adept at getting cigarettes or chewing gum off the visitors, which they 'traded' in the classroom. Suddenly, 'Lucky Strike', Camel', 'Chestertons' and 'Old Gold' cigarette brand names became common parlance. I really don't remember any smoking taking place in the confines of the school but elsewhere the activity was clearly enjoyed. Apparently the nearby Knyfton's woods was a venue for a smoke. Chewing gum was sold and exchanged, whilst nylon stockings were also traded but on a different 'market'. The role in life, of which we were only just beginning to learn, of what we now more familiarly call condoms (the Americans called them thus even then, but 'French letters' was the more common term for us), was progressed by supplies from the US forces, normally only to be used as balloons. There was little else for us to do with them. There are reports of the boys letting these 'balloons' purposefully drift over to the girls side of the playing field. When the 'french letters' turned up in our Scout bivouacs in Knyftons Woods it was a bit of a surprise and in a subsequent write-up, I see that I have called them, delicately, ' the debris of love making'. Joe Louis, the famous heavy weight boxer, presented a boxing event for US Forces on Weston's recreation ground and a number of pupils (particularly those in the ATC) attended that. General Eisenhower came just before D-day on a morale boosting visit to troops in the south-west and stayed overnight in a caravan parked near the water tower in Weston woods. In recent years a friend found some American veterans photographing a seemingly uninteresting bit of ground near the tower and when asked why, they said, 'that's where General Eisenhower addressed us'.

Individual initiatives led to an improvement in our 'scoutcraft'. One pupil I recall was quite adept at tracking US visitors with their girl friends in Weston woods so that he...well, use your imagination. Peter Weaver, in turn, recalls playing at commandos up in the woods with three or four friends, blacking their faces near dusk, and entering the American lines with the intent of relieving them of some of their K rations which contained all sorts of enjoyable edible goodies - seems a bit hairy, to me.

But suddenly they were all gone - en route, by different ways to Normandy. For quite a few, their last days of any sort of happiness might well have been in Weston-super-Mare.

With their going, there was quite a lot of bric-a-brac left over in the premises that they had occupied, and it seemed there for the picking. For many years I worked on my studies at a US Army field desk, that somehow we acquired at that time. It was only within the last year or so, (60 years later) that I gave it to a WW2 buff, who lives opposite.
Weston saw very little of the US Army Air Force, being well to the west of their principal theatre of operations. There were just a few occasions when large squadrons of 'B-17 Flying Fortresses' and 'B-29 Liberators' flew over or near Weston, on missions principally to U-boat bases in occupied France. One battle damaged 'Fortress' landed at Weston Airport, a trials 'Lancaster' normally parked at the end of the runway being moved to facilitate this landing. I was over there not long after it landed. I still have a note of its identification ' C-29524-K, call sign VK-K and named 'Meat Hound'. It was the stuff of being a schoolboy during that era. 'Meat Hound' appears to have eventually come to grief on 11th January 1944.

ROLL OF HONOUR

At its dedication in 1953, the Boys School War Memorial contained the names of 55 boys and one master who had died in the armed forces during the second World War. Only four of the boys had been at the school in the forties and then, nor surprisingly, very early on.

Since virtually none were known to us and perhaps because casualties were too readily accepted as the inevitable result of war, the regular listing of their names in the school magazine, and their sometimes mention at Assembly, bought forward relatively little response or sadness. To me, it all seems much more poignant now.
The first old boy to have been killed in action was C.A.G. Baker who had left the school in 1931. Casualties listed in the school magazine slowly increased in number and eight were listed in both in 1942 and 1943. Later, people earlier listed as 'Missing' were confirmed as being killed. A large percentage of these casualties were members of the Royal Air Force Volunteer Reserve and were flying as air crew. A number of past pupils were listed as prisoners-of-war.

One of our girl pupils at the time, has since recalled that two of the three boys in her road who lost their lives on active service, were County School boys. 'I look back now and realise how there seemed to be no outward emotion reflecting their families' distress. Life had to go on' she reflects.

But the majority were relatively young men who gave their lives in a cause that at that time, and hopefully subsequently, we all believed in. We must never forget that.

There does not appear to be a comprehensive list of medals or decorations awarded to past school pupils.

A number of past members of the girls school joined the women's services but there appears to be little mention of them and no evidence that any lost their lives. Miss Farthing in an entry in the School magazine expressed the intent to assemble a record of all the girls' school past pupils' involvement in the war effort, but if it was ever done no one appears to know what happened to it.

But indeed, they also served.

FOOD AND SCHOOL MEALS

The school had a very well equipped kitchen, as part of the hall complex. For many years the caretaker's wife, Mrs Dowdell presided in this kitchen, in a very professional manner. School dinners were in being before the war but some say only a minority took them. One view was that at 9d a day, they may have been deemed expensive, whilst a contrary view is that 'having lunch at school was quite unusual in those days and was really reserved for the pupils that came by train from Clevedon and elsewhere, and, dare I say it, for the "poor children"'. (This informant didn't seem to like evacuees either). Most pupils either took sandwiches or went home. Those who did the former, had to go and sit in the (separated) halls and there was a charge, remembered to be about 2/- per term, for the use of the table linen. June Hale who joined the school in 1937 remembers 'good plain food' being served which inevitably changed with the onset of the war. She remembers white blancmange served with jam sauce, a sort of sweet batter nicknamed 'mattress' and another pudding called 'dead man's leg'.

Half day schooling then probably put paid to school dinners. They were certainly reintroduced later, probably in 1943 Some recall that when the dinners were reinstated, the first course and the second course were served on alternate days - perhaps whilst the kitchen was 'working up'. Even then it was not all plain sailing, for my diary for 11th June 1945, and for the day after, reads 'Went school but couldn't have school dinners because of shortage. So came home.'

The recollection of the quality of the meals is that they were very variable, but the constraints must have been colossal. Certainly the kitchen produced an excellent 'spotted Dick' steam pudding, but semolina and its consistency raised doubts. In its pink form it was apparently known as 'communist pudding' at the outset of the Cold War. Roy Peacock remembers sausages being on the menu ' but they were minute, about one and a half inches long, and two per boy'. Marion Davies recalls that the worst dinner was a slice of corn beef, a scoop of Pom, cold beetroot and with cold beetroot juice over the Pom. Pom, a wartime powdered mash potato to be reconstituted on site was probably the first mass industrial feeding product introduced into school meals. Until then all vegetables were freshly cooked on the premises. 'Choice' wasn't a word in the culinary dictionary, at that time. The costs of the meals had to be met on a weekly basis, seemingly remembered by some as 5d, 7d or 9d each depending on parental means. Others cannot remember any means-related charges for anything, whilst they were at the school. In the case of the boys (as ever, there was no mixing with the girls), duty monitors collected the food from the kitchens and dispensed it from tables set up in boys' half of the school hall. I remember that later in 1943 the more worldly of our colleagues who had close connections with the US forces, called these dispensing tables, the 'chow line'.

The one abiding recollection shared by nearly all partakers was that you were encouraged (some say, had) to eat everything that was on your plate, 'because there's a war on'. Any reluctance, at least on the girls' side might be met by a tap on the knuckles with a soup ladle, recalls Marion Davies. Jean Innes additionally recalls that her mother reminded her that 'people in India and China were starving'. Jean says, to this day, she cannot see food wasted. Freda Star was told off for the way she held her fork. Two masters were normally on duty in the boys hall and they would have disapproved of any leftovers on the plates.
The other aspects of corporate feeding were school milk and school buns, or their like. Throughout the state educational system, pupils were supplied with 1/3rd pint bottles of milk, at the morning break. The milk variously seemed to be free, or maybe halfpenny a bottle. Someone has recalled that Miss Farthing used to take home any milk left in the bottles, for her cats. Then there were school buns also available at

morning break time at a penny each. These were very much on a 'one per person' basis. I was one of those who at one time dispensed these buns in the boys wash room. We collected them in a big tray from the kitchen but I never thought of asking if these were the products of Mrs. Dowdell's skill or whether they were bought in from a local baker. Although delightful in the short term they quite quickly became somewhat stale. Others recall that early in the war, Mars bars were also sold at morning break.

By late in 1945, on average, 130 boys were having school dinners, 200 were taking milk and 240 were buying a bun, each day, out of a school complement which would have been about 320.

School dinners have to be seen in the context of the food rationing environment in which all pupils had to live. Undoubtedly, people living in the country areas fared better than those who lived in the towns but overall, the majority, including country folk, got by on the rations that they were allowed. Detractors of those times will always assure you that the black market was rife but that was not my experience. Thus school dinners did help in the overall plan of things. Although the rations per adult changed slightly as the war progressed, the core content was typically, milk 3 pints; sugar 8oz.; tea 2oz; butter 2 oz; margarine 4 oz; cheese 3 oz; bacon 4 oz and meat to the value of 1/2d - all per adult, per week. Sweets were rationed from 1942 to 1953, and there was a short period towards the end of the war when the manufacture of ice-cream was banned. Bread was rationed for about two years from 1946, that is after the war, with the introduction of B.U's - bread units. Various tinned foods were covered by a points system which allowed a certain individual discretion as to what to buy with a relatively meagre allocation of 'points'. Only bread and jam came off ration before the end of the 1940s. Butter, cheese, margarine, cooking fats and meat, did not come off ration until 1954. Fresh vegetables were never rationed - but the choice could be minimal and people were encouraged to grow their own. Sausages were not rationed but were often difficult to obtain. They were often saved 'under the counter' for regular customers. Fish was not rationed but supplies were far from plentiful. It was an era of improvisation. Alison Day remembers making sweets - 'chocolate kisses' - from grated raw potato, cocoa and sugar. As she says - 'Ugh'.

Overall it seems quite surprising that most pupils led a very active life and participated in a lot of sporting activity on what by today's standards, looks like very meagre fare, indeed. In fact, post-war studies have suggested that we were never healthier.

THE 'HOUSES'

Both the Girls and the Boys had a house system. There had been, in the 'thirties, a Government encouraged policy of introducing a 'house' system in to the State sector similar in intent to that which had been established in 'Public' Schools, for many years. Normally a four house system appeared to be the norm, but both the girls and the boys at Broadoak Road initially had a three house system and shared the same names - no doubt a throwback to the Nithsdale Road days. This arrangement of three house was probably influenced by the fifteen players in a rugby team, for with both Junior and Senior levels of play, four houses would have needed 120 active players to have serviced the inter-house rugby competition. The girls in the earlier mixed school seem to have had to follow suit and then retained that arrangement at the new Broadoak Road school. So there were three houses, 'Alfred' (Blue), 'Arthur'(Red) and 'Dunstan'(Green), for the whole school - girls and boys. However it seems that the girls started afresh after the June '42 air raid and their new magazine, 'The Phoenix', was soon reporting on the happenings of four houses, having commented that three houses made for 'very big' houses. They were now named 'Arden' (gold), 'Rossendale'(red), 'Savernake'(blue) and 'Sherwood' (green). However, the change didn't appear to have everyone's approval for there was a plaint in the school magazine that 'many Seniors regretting the passing of the former houses, did not make all the effort they could, to cooperate'. Perhaps it was the breaking down of old allegiances that caused this rift.

The principal competitive component of the house system was sport - netball, hockey, rounders, swimming and tennis for the girls and rugby, cricket and athletics including cross-country running, and later gym and swimming (which was reintroduced in 1946), for the boys. However the girls also competed in drama and singing seemingly from the outset, whilst a drama component was added to the boys' competitive activity by the end of the decade. The girls' houses also showed pleasure at the individual successes of their members in such competitions as oratory, elocution, essays and domestic science. The award of cups and shields to the winning houses, was always a major component of any Speech Day.

The girls at one time had a wild flower competition but on an *inter-form* basis, based on who could collect the greatest number of species, an activity that would now no doubt be discouraged. The quadrangle greenhouse was the venue for this event.

With the 'non-competitive' ethos of recent education policy, the house system seems to have faded away in the State system, but in a new policy statement, the Government in 2004, has indicated an intention to re-introduce 'houses' to state schools. For us in the 1940s it was the norm and the perceived evil of competition, was to us an unknown consideration. To some, particularly the boys, competition was probably what life was all about, and it had a relevance comparable to some of the academic study.

Had we known of this later attitude towards non-competition, we would have probably considered to be a lot of old baloney.

SCHOOL MAGAZINES

Both the girls and the boys had a school magazine. The girls original version appears to have been simply called 'Magazine' and was associated with the County School. It was relaunched some time after the June '42 air raid, as 'The Phoenix', under the banner of the Grammar School. The boys' magazine was called 'The Westonian' and it maintained a sort of continuity throughout the 1940s. The girls magazine seems to have been an annual publication, whilst the boys attempted two editions per year.

Both magazines had a staple diet of school match reports and news of old girls or old boys, along with examination successes. The boys then seemed to cover happenings at the school with a certain thoroughness, whilst the girls magazine carried more literary and

comic contributions from pupils, as well as descriptions of events that individuals had enjoyed, such as 'My first flight' (Weston-Cardiff), and the 'June '46 victory celebrations in London'. The boys' magazine did carry some individual literary contributions, but it additionally had to find space for reports on the Scouts and on the ATC. Many of the contributions from pupils, particularly from the girls, were interesting and very witty.

The boys magazine carried advertisements at each end of the publication. Inevitably Wm. Burrow Ltd. of Meadow Street, the largest of the official school outfitters led the field, whilst John Moore and Stead and Simpson also made a pitch for items of clothing or footwear. There was also a wide range of others hoping to catch the eye of the casual browser, or perhaps more likely to be willing to contribute financially to the magazine's production. Grocers, watchmakers, electrical and wireless suppliers, confectioners and furnishers all advertised in the magazine. But the most interesting was a family chemist in Moorland Road, who offered 'The Three Syrups Tonic' claiming it to be 'the right remedy when you are feeling run down from overwork, worry and mental strain'. Just the thing for your average County School pupil.

Advertising finished in September 1943, the first boys' school magazine to be produced after Mr Price joined the school. Maybe it was a paper shortage - maybe not.

EXTERNAL AGENCIES

On reflection, and as far as pupils were concerned, there appears to have been very little involvement with external agencies in terms of the day-to-day running of the school. There was for instance, no Parent-Teacher association, although a Parent Association was formed in 1946. As we have seen, parents might be invited to attend upon the headmistress or headmaster in the face of their child's misdemeanour, but other than that, parent involvement was almost confined to the annual Speech Day, to Sports Day (for the boys) and for a hardy few, their occasional presence on the touchline of a rugby match. Parents did probably seek the occasional audience with the Head in respect ofchild's progress or future, but one senses that these were quite rare occasions. One feels that we were quite resilient souls in those days and paddled our own way through much of the system. On principle alone, I would not have welcomed any *regular* involvement of my parents, with the school. Having said that, my father did intervene decisively three times in my education during the 1940s, twice as a result of exigencies arising from the war, but once with Mr Price, when my father requested that he have me back for a third year in the sixth after I left without contemplating a University career. I have acknowledged these in my own personal recollections.

The main events that *did* involve parents, were the annual Speech Days. Both the boys and the girls had their separate days. They were definite

*Limbering up for the Sicilian Tarantella Dance
for the girls Speech Day - 1948.*

occasions, run to a fairly standard format. This was the occasion when the dividing wall between the two halves of the school hall was wound back, the other school was given the afternoon off, and the hall was set out for the whole school, their parents and friends. Teachers and Governors sat in their finest array on the stage, with teachers wearing their academic gowns and the colourful hoods of their various Universities. The principal task of distributing prizes and honours was performed by a visiting luminary who normally had religious or academic leanings. This luminary then addressed the gathered multitude in a manner that could occasionally be quite amusing or instructive, and just occasionally, both. Early in the 1940s the boys school choir performed on these occasions and the Air Training Corps cadets and the Scouts were inspected by the dignitaries, but these elements lapsed as the war progressed. In the post war years, a 'display of work' began to creep in, and the girls began to entertain their guests with dancing but save that, the visitors didn't get much farther than the school hall. Any mass involvement was confined to the singing of the National Anthem and the School Hymn. Normally, no refreshments were offered. One aspect of Speech Day that set it aside albeit in a fairly insignificant manner, was that we saw the School Governors. What their precise role was, I never did gather and to this day, I can only surmise. Their deliberations were never publicly published. Never in my time at the school did I ever speak with one, I never knowingly saw one alongside the rugby field of athletic track; I am sure none ever visited the Scout Troop. However, no doubt they did a good job, and this disconnect was undoubtedly typical of all manner of quasi-official relationships, in those days. Over the years, quite a number of the school magazines started with an expression of regret by the Headmaster or Headmistress, at the death or departure of one or other school governor, but in the absence of any awareness of their being, it was difficult for the rest of us, to feel their passing.

I do not think as pupils we had any concept of a local education authority, although something of that form was housed in offices in Walliscote Road. The overall feeling that I am left with is of a school under its own autonomous management largely in the hands of the Headmistress or Headmaster, influenced externally only by the requirements of the examination boards at, as it happened, Oxford and Bristol. A more mature view could no doubt put these aspects of the school's existence into better context, for as pupils at the time we never considered such issues as the provision of resources or the financial management of the school. These were taken as given.

SPORT

The Girls

Miss Farthing was opposed to athletics for girls -whether for aesthetic, propriety or physical reasons is not clear. However the girls' school pursued team games with considerable vigour, - hockey, netball, rounders and tennis, all featured among school teams, and the facilities for them were very good. Swimming continued to offer scope for individual prowess, but for this, pupils had to get to Knightstone baths,

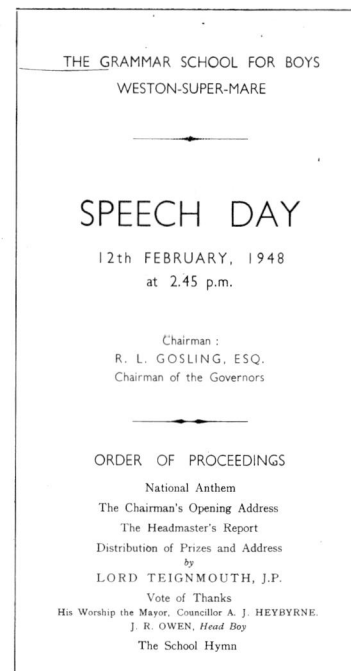

THE GRAMMAR SCHOOL FOR BOYS
WESTON-SUPER-MARE

SPEECH DAY

12th FEBRUARY, 1948
at 2.45 p.m.

Chairman :
R. L. GOSLING, ESQ.
Chairman of the Governors

ORDER OF PROCEEDINGS

National Anthem
The Chairman's Opening Address
The Headmaster's Report
Distribution of Prizes and Address
by
LORD TEIGNMOUTH, J.P.
Vote of Thanks
His Worship the Mayor, Councillor A. J. HEYBYRNE,
J. R. OWEN, *Head Boy*
The School Hymn

which even by school bus was very time consuming However, in Molly Tancock, who was the school's swimming champion for the four years

Girls did not seem to go in for official pictures as did the boys. This is a form hockey team - Form 5W in 1948

up to 1946, the School had , at one time, England's fastest woman swimmer.

The beginning of a new era. New clothing and an official photo in 1950

It seems that for much of the war years, matches were still played against schools elsewhere in Somerset, and Taunton, Bruton, Sidcot and Wells all featured in the fixtures for hockey, tennis and netball, although the Somerset schools league for hockey, was suspended for the duration in 1941. Locally there were games against the private schools of Rossholme, Burton House and Westcliffe, and for a while there were matches against Mitcham and Barking Abbey. The rather forthright comments on some individual performances, in the school magazine are quite an eye opener. Full names were given but I shall settle for initials only. Among the Hockey 1st XI, B.B was 'still not very consistent....too slow in taking opportunities'; B.G 'relied too much on playing with one hand'; P.D 'did not pass soon enough'; J.K 'was a little slow on her feet' whilst B.T 'could sometimes shoot sooner'. Of course there were also many positive comments but they do not make such good reading.

Besides inter-school matches, there were inter-house matches which could raise even more passion. Most interhouse rivalry was resolved on the games field and if the reports in the school magazine are anything to go by, congratulations or exhortations to do better followed success or failure. 'In the swimming sports we again came down badly and we easily took bottom place' lamented the scribe for Sherwood House in 1947. In the same year the Rossendale correspondent expressed the view that they 'should not be discouraged by their position this year; they should be spurred to higher achievements in the future' However there is always a winner and that year it was Savernake. 'The spirit of Savernake is excellent, and the energy and determination of its members have been rewarded by the winning of the school shield' read their report. Educationalists later in the century would have been aghast at this overt intention to win.

The Boys

The Boys' school, consistent with the West Country tradition, was a rugby school. There was no facility or intent to play soccer. Cricket of course was the summer game, whilst cross country running in the Easter Term, and athletics in the Summer Term completed the core sports activity. Swimming was not resumed until 1946.

At rugby, the school played against quite a number of schools that involved a measure of travel - City of Bath School, Dr. Morgans at Bridgwater, and Cotham, Q.E.H , St Brendans, Bristol Grammar and Bristol Cathedral School all in Bristol, as well as Sidcot School and

i) School Cricket 1st XI - 1948

ii) School 1st XV v The Old Boys in 1949
   - a group covering the whole of the 1940s

iii) School Rugby 1st XV - 1947/48

iv) Boys Sixth form, 1946, with F. R.Price

Taunton School. A number of these fixtures involved both a 1st XV and a 2nd XV.

During most of the war years, Mr White, who would have been the guiding light for the school's rugby was in the Forces, but W. J. (Bill) Davies who had played for Somerset RFC in earlier days and Mr. Thomas, filled much of the breach and in no small measure it was down to them, that a good standard of play was achieved throughout that difficult period. Other masters were probably dragooned into being the occasional referee. Reports in the school magazine could be quite pithy.

Various people were landed with observations such as 'he showed a tendency to drop passes and must learn to keep his eye on the ball, not the opponent'; 'in attack he has not come up to expectations'; 'was too frequently tackled in possession'; 'he must learn to part with the ball'; 'a little less fancy work and more speed would make him a first rate full back'. Honest, if nothing else.

Cricket saw matches against roughly the same opponents, not only by the 1st XI, but additionally by a 2nd XI and Colts side and to a lesser extent a Junior XI. Again, house matches were keenly fought. It is interesting that all written comments about the cricket players performance was most gentlemanly compared with the near acid remarks afforded those who played rugby - often the same people, of course .

There was no embargo on the boys having athletics, and the annual sports day was quite an event. Most of the events until the post war era were conventional track events up to 1 mile, along with the long jump and the high jump. Anyone who possessed a pair of spiked running shoes was rare and very lucky indeed. They were normally shared around any friends who had roughly the same size feet. It was only later, that the javelin, shot and discus were introduced. Again, aside from individual prowess, the main competing element was inter-house rivalry.

Post war, a triangular athletics competition was established with Huish's School at Taunton and Dr. Morgan's School from Bridgwater, in which Weston normally did quite well. Individuals also participated in the County Youth sports at Taunton, although this time they were running for the town. I got four days leave from the Army before I had even joined (for National Service), to run the 880 yds for Weston, at Taunton in July 1948. The other element of the boys' athletics was the cross-country. There were four grades by age with the senior course being quite a challenge. It went from the school, up through Hutton woods on to Bleadon Hill, down around the back and over the hill at Uphill and then along the sands. Just as tiredness was really setting in, you were confronted by the loose dry sand of the sand dunes which could be very wearying indeed. Then the skill if you were in the lead, was to judge your pace so as to get back to school just as the girls were emerging at the end of their day.

The boys' school athletic team at Taunton - 1949

When swimming was reintroduced in 1946, because of the shortness of time and the long way that they had to travel to Knightstone baths, some boys wore their presumably fairly tight swimming trunks under their normal trousers. These became extremely uncomfortable and one has confirmed that they were hard put to concentrate on the lessons that preceded the swimming. For success in all these endeavours, 'colours' were awarded to the best performing individuals in all the sports. At least for the boys, this permitted the wearing of the school badge on their sports vest, particularly in rugby and athletics, aside from a certificate presented on Speech Day.

The photo above depicts travel in a modern coach, but for many years round about the end of the war, the boys travelled in a venerable canvas roofed, drafty 'charabanc' - 'The Silver Queen' - run by Don Williams, an old boy of the school.

Although 'visits' were severely curtailed during the war, lectures on various topics to both schools featured throughout the decade. At their core were a series of lectures, known as the Wyndham lectures, funded by a school benefactor. They nearly always had a local, or at least an historical, theme. Topics embraced subjects such as 'The Romans on Mendip', 'Caves of Mendip', 'King Alfred', 'Cathedrals' and more general topics such as 'The Stone Ages', 'The Industrial Revolution' and 'Medieval Man'. A talk, somewhat out of that genre, entitled 'A survey of world affairs' based on the figure of Ernest Bevin was considered to be 'most instructive'. I recall that a sum of money was set aside for the projectionists (that is, he who worked the magic lantern) a role that I willingly performed at one stage for a fee of 1/6d per occasion.

There were other lectures, often to bring an awareness to some society or to some good cause. A talk on the CPRE (Council for the Preservation of Rural England) set some of the girls into a very ardent support for saving rural England and wore badges proclaiming that intent. The plight of African babies caused them to make woollen flower button holes to sell to each other, in order to raise money. Lectures followed on topics such as 'Road Safety', 'Nursing as a profession' 'Life in Occupied France' and many others. There were talks in support of Dr Barnardo's Homes, the RSPCC and the RSPCA.

During the war, the boys, particularly the seniors, had lectures with a forces recruitment dimension, sometimes on the basis of a talk on a recent campaign. On perhaps three occasions the lecture was followed by a fairly substantial exhibition of army equipment and weapons on the school playing field. To be able to simply talk across the field by radio bought forth an interest that is hardly believable today. Roy Perry recalls that one soldier equipped with climbing irons on his legs climbed the school flag pole, to the general disquiet of Mr. Price. Occasionally old boys on forces leave, talked to the senior boys.

The Wyndham fund also financed visits, on themes generally similar to those of the lectures. There were none during the war but they recommenced in October 1945 when the boys' second forms were taken to Dolbury Camp and the Roman amphitheatre at Charterhouse. The girls went to Montecute House.

Visits on more general themes came about with both the girls' and the boys' seniors going (separately) to the Long Ashton agricultural

research station and to the Atomic Energy exhibition at Bristol (Temple Meads).

The girls went to the pathological lab. at Weston Hospital, the Cellophane factory at Bridgwater, to the Old Mixon factory when by then the production was of prefabricated houses (and no longer Bristol 'Beaufighters), Robertsons jam factory in Bristol, and to the Avonmouth Docks. The boys managed to squeeze in a visit to a coal mine at Radstock. It was quite a primitive mine (at least by later standards) with open acetylene cap lamps, and peoples' main recollections seem to be the drop down the mine shaft and the crack of old roof props. Roy Peacock left his cap down the mine. I don't think any of us saw it as a future career.

There were also more cultural visits, particularly for the girls. Bristol's 'Theatre Royal' was visited fairly regularly to see professional productions of Shakespeare plays, as was the local Knightstone Theatre where local amateur dramatic groups put on plays of a fairly classic type to a high standard. The girls' 'Balletomaniacs' as they chose to call themselves, also went to performances of the ballet in Bristol. The Odeon cinema was visited to see 'Nicholas Nickleby'.

All this relates primarily to the two or three years after the war. This whole aspect of school life probably became more significant with time after that.

16TH WESTON-SUPER-MARE GIRL GUIDE COMPANY

Marian Hale recalls that in 1942, during her second year at the County School, Miss Newman-Phillips, the schools domestic science teacher announced that she was re-forming an old established Guide company, the '16th Weston-super-Mare', which had almost ceased to exist. She recruited quite a number of the younger girls into the Company including Marian and a number of her classmates and friends. Although some girls from other schools joined it, it became almost a County school company, so much so, that on occasions the school magazine carried news of its happenings. They met on Friday evenings in the Congregational Church hall in Moorland Road and did 'Girl Guide' type things. Miss Philips proved to be a popular Guide captain, and on at least two occasions in the post war years she organised Guide camps for her company. One was to Oxwich on the Gower Peninsular in Wales and another at Bicknoller in the Quantocks. They slept on ground sheets on the ground, the only additional comfort being a scooped-out hollow in the soil to cater for their hips. Sleeping bags were home made and assiduously searched for creepy crawlies, each night. Other aspects of creature comforts were correspondingly primitive. The contrasting highlights were the Christmas parties, particularly as some were jointly held with the School scouts and, to ensure that we, the school scouts, didn't think that we had any proprietary rights, also with the Scouts of

Guides on their way to their summer camp at Bicknoller in 1947

3rd Weston (St.Pauls). As Marian has commented, 'looking back, this was quite an innovation considering how segregated we were at school, and additionally surprising because 'we always considered Miss Philips to be rather shy'. Many lasting relationships started as a result of those innocent social events' *and*, I should add, the walk home after the Guides and the School Scouts had finished near about the same time, on Friday evenings.

Other girls at the school attended other Guide companies in the town - particularly with the company that met in what was universally known as the 'Guide Hut' above Grove Park. Janet Lovell (Owen) remembers being the patrol leader of the Fuschia Patrol - a 'stupid name' as she now describes it.

17th WESTON-SUPER-MARE (COUNTYSCHOOL) SCOUT TROOP.

There doesn't appear to be a formal record of when the County School Scout Troop was formed, but it was well established by the beginning of

the 'forties. By mid-1940, there were 32 scouts in the troop, established in four patrols with, by today's standards, the rather un-cool names of, Foxes, Penguins, Ravens and Starlings. It met normally on a Friday evening in the rather austere environment of the school hall, but even

At Bicknoller

this was after a period when the troop met in the Scout Hut on the playing field. This hut was really only man enough to store some heavy baggage and the troop's activities had been severely limited. The hall was a vast improvement. But, it was not a very 'Scouty' atmosphere - no flag raising, nothing 'Scouty' on the walls, and unlike our (for I was a one of the Scouts) friendly rivals - 3rd (St. Pauls), we didn't have a band. However, the local benefactor, Mrs. Graves-Knyfton permitted us access to part of her estate, the 'Plantation' just across the Uphill Road from the school, and that's where we could exercise axemanship, tracking, stalking and other backwoodsman type of activity. Alas, the school hall did dominate most meetings but the option of the Plantation during the summer months was a very welcome alternative.

The principal activities on a Friday evening were generally towards progress in the Scout hierarchy - from Tenderfoot, to Second Class, and then to First Class Scout. They embraced all the attributes associated with Scouting - knots, first aid, camping, cooking, map reading etc. Proficiency badges were largely at the discretion or interest of the individual and there was a substantial list of outside examiners to cater for the more unusual. With a certain combination of the appropriate badges you could become a 'King's Scout'. However there were fairly regular, particularly post-war, courses which lead to proficiency badges including 'Meteorology' under the guidance of George White, and 'Fireman' following instruction at the principal Weston fire station, then on Beach Road. This culminated in a Friday evening visit to the headquarters of No 17 Fire Force at the Bridewell Fire Station in Bristol, when a full scale false alarm was put on for our benefit. I am pretty sure (later, yes it was) that it was on the day that Mahatma Gandhi was assassinated - 30th January 1948. Funny, how you remember these things.

Nr.Bridgwater, at the end of July 1940. It was fairly near the beach, and a wide range of scouts pursuits were followed. A final camp fire was not possible, but Lord St Audries, on whose estate they were camped, provided the use of 'electrically lit' barn and the final singsong and sketches seemed to have been thoroughly enjoyed by all those who attended. Later, there were fairly small (patrol) camps, besides the principal camps which at that time were the Farming Camps. These are dealt with elsewhere. I remember Bobby Rigg's 'Owl' patrol, hauling a decorators cart from his home in Walliscote Road to Shiplate in June 1943, for a short patrol camp. Later the Seniors hauled the trek-cart that the troop had by then acquired to Christon, for an Easter Camp in 1944. The only other solace, as related above, was our arms length (you can say that again) association with the Moorland Road (16th Weston-super-Mare) Guides who, again as related earlier, were largely members of the Girls' County School. Slowly a number of joint social events took place which eventually lead to providing wives for two of us, (albeit some years later) and near misses for a number of others.

In 1945, the concept of 'Senior Scouts' was introduced presumably to retain the interests of the older (15/16 year old, say) Scout, and the County School Troop then formed a separate patrol of 'Senior Scouts'. Patrol names moved from the avian variety to the

The School Scout Troop in 1944

more heroic, and I recall that we were the 'Orde Wingate' patrol, named after the famed, but alas dead, Chindit leader. I remember that we tried to do more in the line of backwoodsman by trying to light fires without matches and even went hunting adders on the Mendips for reasons that I don't recall as being very praiseworthy. At a Somerset County camp near Wellington, the seniors' programme, included 'a visit to industry'. It just happened to be Wivilescombe brewery. An old gentleman was explaining the beer making process and told us that the mash, whatever, was heated to 80 degrees. 'Would that be Centigrade or Fahrenheit, Sir? asked a technically minded Scout. 'Neither', answered the old boy in strong Somerset accent 'it's 'eat'. There were no other questions.

Camping was a problem during the war, with no fires after dark of course, and even during the day they had their uncertainties. The last true Troop camp until the end of hostilities, was at Stogursey,

In all this sweetness and light, Ivan Armstrong reminds us that there was another side. Having grown out of his Scout shorts which his parents were hard put to replace, Ivan attended a Scout meeting in long trousers. 'We are not cowboys' observed 'Fud' Hill rather critically, so Ivan left and joined the town's Sea Cadets where the uniform was issued free.

On the 18th August 1944, whilst most of us were at the second farming camp at Wanstrow, the troop suffered the tragic loss of one of its members in a bathing tragedy at the mouth of the River Axe at Uphill. Hugh Cunliffe, then aged 13 was bathing with a number of friends, including a personal friend, Brian Hill from Rickmansworth, who was staying with him. They got into difficulties and John Williams, aged 12 at the time, also of the Troop who was with them, was instrumental in saving Hill. Alas, Cunliffe was drowned. For this act of bravery John was awarded the Scout's Silver Cross with Blue ribbon, as well as The Royal Humane Society's 'Parchment of Bravery'. The Scout Silver Cross was presented to him at a ceremony on 6th January 1945. Many of us attended and we were all very proud of him.

The Easter 1948 hike, in the Quantocks

The 'worldwide brotherhood of Scouts' had an uncertain ring about it during the war, but slowly it came about again. In 1946, Derek Porter, John Dyer and Roy Peacock were chosen to represent the troop at a Scandinavian Scout Jamboree, to be held in Sweden. With travelling being so commonplace these days, it is difficult to imagine the awe that this venture engendered, and dare it be said, the sort of envy that simmered in those who weren't going. They went through Denmark, a onetime occupied country, that was seemingly awash in white bread, butter, strawberries, milk and cheese. It left them aghast. Two years later I was to assemble almost the same view about Holland when on my way to National Service, in Germany. In England rationing, and grey coloured bread was still the norm. I suppose the authorities were doing their best. On all sorts of fronts this trip to Scandinavia was an eye opener to those who went.

The turn of others came the following year. In August 1947, Jeff Hynds (representing the YMCA troop), Philip Hoskins (representing Hill Road troop) and I, (representing the Grammar School Troop), all pupils of the school were chosen to be part of the Somerset contingent to the first post war World jamboree (' Jamboree Mondial de la Paix') to be held at Moisson, near Paris. Perhaps not quite so exotic as Scandinavia, it was still an occasion, an experience, way beyond that of the average young person, at that time. To have even been to Paris in those days, set you aside. However, I wrote that before I read in a copy of the last School Magazine before the war, a comment on one of two fellow form members who had indeed, been to Paris that year (1939). It said rather acidly 'he has been distributing his knowledge most generously ever since'. I hope that we weren't that bad.

From 24th July to 7th August 1947, the School troop held its first, post-war, annual (non-farming camp) Scout camp. It was held at Bossington, on the Somerset coast, near Porlock. The realities of those times led to Mr Hill circulating all parents with a note saying that the double rations that had been enjoyed at the farming camps would not prevail at this camp. They were asked if they could spare a 'little extra of one or more of

The Patrol Leaders in 1945

the following commodities - tea, tinned foods, fats, sugar, jam or marmalade, coarse soap or soap flakes'. Understandably, food parcels to individual Scouts were actively discouraged. It turned out to be a most enjoyable camp.

Even apart from these isolated highlights, what is so memorable is the friendship and camaraderie that these very simple Scouting pleasures engendered. Quite a number of members of the troop are still in contact, sixty years later.

In all this recollection, save a passing reference, there has been no mention of the Scoutmasters that led the troop. I leave that till last. The Scoutmaster who most will associate with the Troop at that time is H.C.Wood - a master who taught French at the School (but, by chance, never me). Even to this day I don't know his Christian name. To all the Scouts he was 'Skipper' or 'Skip'. (It seemed amusing that my computer's spelling checker didn't like 'H.C.Wood' and I had to click on 'skip' to proceed). He seemed youngish and approachable, and set the tone of the Troop. 'Fud' Hill, the History master, somewhat more austere, had been the Scoutmaster in earlier days and had moved on to an Area role, but now assisted H.C.Wood. From outside the school, Mr V.E.C. Berkeley who had or had had, three sons at the school, was officially an ASM - an Assistant Scout Master. Then

'Skip' - Mr. H. C. Wood

H.C Wood left the School, and Mr Hill stepped into the breach that was probably difficult to fill from the other schoolmasters at that time. Without him, the troop might have faltered. So on it went. I feel totally indebted, perhaps not adequately appreciated at the time, to these gentlemen who gave up so much of their time, for the good of so many young people. In 1948, Mr Isaacs, joined the school and became active with the Scouts. A note comments that his wartime jungle training was most useful. I am somewhat short of the troop's history after that, but a new era was represented by the Troops summer camp being held in Kandersteg, in the Bernese Oberland, in 1949, and the Troop Report in the School magazine of April 1953, was recording that ' We hope to dip into our waiting list fairly soon, as there are many boys yearning to join our ranks'

THE AIR TRAINING CORPS - 159 SQUADRON

The school's Air Training Corps Unit had its origins in a unit of the Air Defence Cadet Corps formed at the school on 25th July 1939, with the headmaster, Mr T. E. Lindfield as Officer Commanding. By September

An inspection of 159 Squadron on the school playing field.

it had 8 officers (not all from the school) and 56 cadets, with Mr J. R. Hay, (the Chemistry master) as the adjutant. By the time that the squadron was embraced by the Air Training Corps Scheme, Mr Hay was the Commanding Officer. Recruitment was not entirely from the school, and by January 1942 it had a strength of about 100 cadets. In both its ADCC and ATC forms, its designation was, No 159 Squadron. The squadron enjoyed a wide range of instruction, on such subjects as the 'theory of flight', the working of the internal combustion engine, and aircraft rigging, at RAF Locking.

Nearer home there was instruction on signalling, first aid, map reading, theory of navigation etc. Quite a number of the school's teachers assisted with this instruction, including, Bill Davies (signalling, and electricity and magnetism), George White (map reading) and 'Snug' Robinson (the internal combustion engine). Other instruction was given by local RAF personnel. A Vickers 'Vildebeest' biplane was delivered and positioned alongside the ATC hut on the school playing field, and Ted Johnson has even been able to furnish its RAF serial number -

K6398. It was taken on charge by the school's squadron, on 6th December 1940. Some recall that its wings were stored in the ATC hut and there are a number of references of it being eventually disposed of, when local residents thought that it might indicate the presence of an airfield, to the Luftwaffe. Others have contested this notion but no date for its removal seems to have survived.

As the squadron matured, annual camps at RAF and RN air stations were a regular feature and flying as passengers in RAF aircraft became

F/O J. R. Hay leading 159 Squadron ATC.

fairly common. Gus Fletcher remembers a flight in an Airspeed 'Oxford' from Lulsgate, a flight which made a temporary landing on Bath racecourse followed immediately on his return to Lulsgate by an unscheduled flight in another Oxford when, to his surprise, the pilot assumed the role of proving that a newly fitted wing actually was fixed quite securely. Fortunately it proved so to be, despite the pilot's endeavours. Gus is also willing to reveal, under pressure, the name of a school cadet who contrived to raise the undercarriage of a Bristol Beaufighter at Filton whilst it was on the ground. Damage was assessed at £100.

Gliding instruction was also on offer towards the end of the war on Weston airfield, the home of No. 87 Gliding School. Mr Robinson who had been very active with 159 Squadron on his return from a wartime training responsibility, transferred to it, to become adjutant and gliding instructor. 'He was very dedicated to it, nothing was too much trouble and we had a great time' recalls Graeme Forrester .

The principle aim of the ATC was acknowledged to be 'the provision a steady stream (of recruits) for the services', primarily the RAF of course. The school magazine in early 1942 records 14 cadets who had

'been called for Service' in the previous year. It also listed six onetime cadets who were undergoing training as pilots at that time. The Squadron obviously met this principle aim.

However with the cessation of hostilities it seems that the fortunes of the unit faltered for a while before picking up again in the 1950s.

THE SCHOOL SOCIETIES

In the era of the shared school (with Barking Abbey and Mitcham), many extra curricular activities were badly effected by sheer lack of space, or indeed, any place to meet at all. However, albeit slowly, various school societies were reformed under the enthusiasm normally of a teacher and then of the pupils themselves.

A seemingly short lived one was the Girls 'Science Club'. This was formed early in 1948, and 'the making of bath salts and fireworks proved overwhelmingly popular'. Invisible ink was also on the calendar. Images of St. Trinians follow naturally. The club began to falter at the suggestion of a science exhibition when 'the girls discovered that to prepare such an exhibition that had to think and do things for themselves..... instead of having entertainment handed out'. This report was not attributed but sounds like a unhappy member of staff, and by the end of summer term, the idea of the club had been abandoned.

At least on the basis of the school magazine reports, the girls overall didn't appear quite so clubable as the boys although they were far more active in competitions for interests such as drama, elocution, singing, gym and wild flowers.

On the other hand the boys slowly assembled a wide range of clubs and societies including, (eventually) a dramatic society, a chess club, a record club, a jazz club and a photographic society.

The Orchestral Society seemed quite buoyant throughout. The society was under the direction of Mr. Thomas, who later in 1942 started additionally, the Music Society which both supplanted and shared the same interests as the orchestral society. Many people of that era, even those who were not members of either society will remember the musical abilities of Leonard Silver, an extremely talented young musician equally at home with both violin and piano. In December 1945 the first school concert for some time was held in the school hall. Soloists particularly mentioned were Mr Thomas (piano), Mr Robinson (violin), Leonard Silver (violin), and A. Christopher (soprano). The school choir sang, and the audience was invited to join in some well known carols. Perhaps it was a fitting end to the first term of peace.

The English Society had a more chequered career, faltering under all sorts of problems, particularly space, but found resurrection when the Moorland Road Hall became available for their meetings. Their staple activities were, spelling bees, debates, general knowledge competitions, impromptu plays and readings from the favourite books of its members. By late 1944 they were getting attendances of up to 60, still occasionally trying to squeeze into a classroom designed for 30. Their 'dream' was to present a play, eventually sublimated when the School Dramatic Society was formed in 1946. The catalyst for all this activity was Mr A. B. Davies.

In the Spring Term of 1945, a Chess Club was inaugurated under the direction of Mr Rue. It was initially limited to the Upper School by the number of chess sets available. A school governor presented a silver cup (the Barclay Cup) to be competed for at a chess tournament to be held each Spring Term, and by the end of the decade the society was well established with at least one player playing for the Weston-super-Mare chess club.

The Stamp Club also reopened in 1945, under the direction of Mr. Harris, seemingly with 'lively interest'. The commercial trading of stamps seemed so keen that a number of meetings outside their regular schedule, had to be held.

By the end of the decade, a record club, a jazz club and a photographic society were added to the list of the Boys' school societies.

The fortunes, in terms of members, for most of these societies did wax and wane, for in some measure they were often competing for the same type of person, who was essentially clubable, or society minded, but who might also be already committed to the Scouts or to the ATC. A willingness to be involved in these extracurricular activities wasn't a universal attribute. Additionally, people who had far to travel were always at a disadvantage when it came to contemplating membership of one of the societies.

However for many, these societies gave pleasure and interest.

HARVEST CAMPS.

In the 1943-1946 era, both the girls and the boys participated in various school initiated camps to help gather in the harvest under the general umbrella of the County War Agricultural Committees. In the case of the Scouts it doubled up as their annual camp.

The Boys' Camps

The Scouts will probably look on their four camps as the core of the activity. There were camps at Wanstrow, south of Frome in Somerset, in 1943 and 1944, and at Fitzhead, some miles beyond Taunton, in 1945 and 1946. The format of the Wanstrow camps was that accommodation was quite 'Scouty', under canvas in bell tents with the luxury of straw filled palliases (well, not too luxurious), all set in the field associated with the village Institute. It was in this hall, a large wooden hut really, that we ate our meals albeit after they had been cooked on open fires in the field.

Raising the Flag. Wanstrow Farming Camp 1943

On both occasions, we travelled to Wanstrow with our bikes in a railway brake/passenger van, which was attached to a Bristol bound train, shunted at Yatton and then connected to a Frome bound train going down the Cheddar Valley line. It was at the height of the war but it was all done in a calm and timely fashion. Bucolic, I think is the word. Once we were settled in at the camp site, individuals were allocated to various farms in the area and on the following day we cycled to our allocated farm. The principal job was helping with the cereal harvest, mainly by standing the cut sheaves into 'stooks' for the crop to dry. It was then generally formed into ricks before eventually being thrashed some time after our departure. Combine harvesters as commonplace machines were decades away. It was quite heavy work for a thirteen year old, as I was at the first camp, but vanity seemed to dictate that we performed our task stripped to the waist so that we would get brown, at the expense of a

Waiting to wash-up at Wanstrow - 1943

myriad of small scratches. Whoever were we trying to impress? Perhaps the real discomfort was allayed by my first experience of truly rough cider. The farms' own staff were sensibly dressed in shirts and the occasional waistcoat. The occasion for some of the worst scratches was when the binder was nearing the end of its task, and cutting the last of the crop. Rabbits which had sort sanctuary in the decreasing standing crop would then make a dash for it and to chase them and catch them was the game. It wasn't a game for me, I am much too squeemish. A final leap to the ground might catch the rabbit, but at the same time you could get very scratched by the stubble. One such casualty was later receiving balm on his chest from one of our lady helpers back at camp, when someone politely observed 'perhaps one day he could do the same

for you, miss' It was a rare acknowledgement that the ladies were of the opposite sex.

Indeed having lady helpers at a Scout camp in those days was a *major* excursion from the norms of those times. We had two ladies to help, well in truth to organise, our meals. They were 'Dusty' Miller, our geography mistress and a Miss N. Bradshaw. They stayed in the local pub. In the School Magazine following the 1943 camp they jointly wrote a piece on their recollections. It might be worth recalling just a bit of that for it for it captures some of the atmosphere of the camp so well.

We prepare vegetables and initiate boys into the mystery of pastry-making [there was a rota of cook's helpers among the Scouts] . As the afternoon wears on, the wood pile is replenished and we snatch a cup of tea before the hordes return. The cooks zero hour draws near - the outside workers must have a large meal on time. They trickle in, a few at a time. Dinner; second and third helpings. Greasy dishes are at last washed up , the cocoa is on and the boys drift into the hut to write or play or listen.

It's dark outside, raining too Time they were in bed. Prayers...settle down quickly ...goodnight all.

And so it was.

This excerpt helps to recall that extra rations were made available for these camps and that being in the country undoubtedly had its own advantages on the food front. The other joy was Namco - National Milk Cocoa. It was not available on the domestic front and was only available in canteens for those on 'war work'. A common reward, even if not a hygienic one, for being on cooks' duty, was that you could dip your wet finger into a large tin of Namco, (it was sweet and chocolatey), and have a very enjoyable lick. Indeed one of the many songs made up around about that time by our more literate colleagues, had the chorus which began

> Toorali, toorali, toorali, ey,
> The Namco is fine and we eat it all day

It was the era of Pom the dried mash potato, referred to earlier in the School Dinners chapter, and the verse went on....

> If sometimes you find that your porridge is thin,
> A packet of Pom is the stuff to put in.

That did actually work.

The second Wanstrow (in 1944), with a party of 32, followed the same pattern but with two concerts in the hall, and evening and weekend cycle rides. The 'workers' seemed to be well appreciated by the farmers and were often the beneficiaries of their hospitality. I was working as a lone helper on a small farm and I was invited to afternoon tea on one of the Sundays. The farmer and his wife were most kind but I recall that their lives were marred by thoughts of their son who was a prisoner of the Japanese.

As one interested in aeroplanes I recall the regular evening southerly departure of aircraft of Bomber Command still with their navigation lights on, and separately, the return of Douglas Dakotas/Skytrains, flying quite low, each towing two Waco CG-4 'Hadrian' gliders bringing them back, presumably empty from Normandy. At Weston we were rather short of such sightings.

Fitzhead in 1945 and 1946 was somewhat different, in that the first camp, and to a lesser extent the second, were in isolated fields some way from the village, and we worked for one farmer - Mr. Beresford of Manor Farm. The virgin state of the first site meant that an advanced party was sent on 24 hours ahead of the main party to erect tents and get some things organised, but the dire weather thwarted this. Only an elementary infrastructure was in place before the main party arrived. Somehow it was learned that the previous users of the bedding and equipment, which had been stored at the farm for a year, had been Harrow School and thus for some unexplained reason the advanced party members assumed the name of 'Harrowbugs' to mark their veteran status, and a definite itch. That first night, we all slept in the only bell tent that we appeared to have successfully erected, and for want of something to do in the candle lit interior we tried to make up epithets for girls that we knew or, more truthfully, knew of. Some twins (but more generally known as '*the*' twins) were accorded, perhaps not too originally, 'double indemnity' whilst another person, who indeed is a stalwart at our reunions nearly 60 years later was accorded 'bandy, but handy'. Thankfully I do not remember any others. We also had a poll on the *desirability* of the same ladies, but the results of that poll remain embargoed for another 60 years. The results do still exist. The atomic bombs were dropped on Hiroshima and Nagasaki, during the first few days of this camp.

The work at Fitzhead, was more varied than Wanstrow. Our jobs embraced hoeing sprouts, harvesting corn damaged by the weather, carting baled hay, lifting potatoes and cabbage planting. In the second year, when we were nearer the village and the farm, this scope was extended to what in the school report was called 'silage work'. This was more colloquially known as 'dung-bunging', 'sxxt shifting', or 'muck spreading'. and its practitioners were quietly shunned by others with less odour pervading roles. A similar fate nearly befell John Dyer but for a different reason. He was probably the only scout at that time who could drive a car, and as a result he was given the plumb job of driving the tractor - a Fergusson. There was a definite difference of opinion as to the rate at which his endeavours should unearth the potatoes that others, in back breaking fashion, had to gather. But we were all friends. Another recollection of the second Fitzhead followed some genuine Scout activity of felling a tree. Permission had been granted. As the tree (it wasn't all that big) was being dragged back to camp for firewood, local youths kept jumping on it impeding its progress. They were chased off by the Scouts, only for one of the locals to trip and crack his collar bone. Retribution was feared and my recollection was that we put on a show at the village hall, by way of contrition. In fact my diary shows that the concert predated the injury by a couple of days so that recollection bit the dust, and there was no retribution. By any objective standards the concert must have been pretty modest, I even remember playing the piano which, in public, I had never done before or since. But there were some funny sketches, a few songs and it went down surprisingly well. My recollection is (I am sure that I am right this time) that a school pupil Watson Price, who was not a Scout, but who had come to Fitzhead with us, was the star of the show. Of course this was long before television got to the West Country and pleasures were far far more simple.

By the following year, 1947, the Scouts resumed more conventional Scout camps.

In 1944, 1945 and 1946 the School, aside from the Scouts, held what was called a 'Harvest Camp' in '44, and an 'Agricultural Camp' in '45 and back to 'Harvest Camp' in '46. All these were at Wanstrow. The first one followed the Scouts and used their equipment. I feel that the Scouts probably quietly held a superior attitude to these 'amateurs', but in fact if there was such an attitude it was ill-founded. The camp however, was beset by bad weather. " 'Mud, mud, mud, nothing but mud...' Like the Chartists in 1848, our enthusiasm was sorely tried by persistent and heavy rain.." read one report. Mr Hay, Mr Davies and Mr Harris are all mentioned in the report but it is no longer clear, at this distance, if they were the masters who we would associate with those names. They don't *sound* like campers - but there was, of course, a local hostelry. However food was cooked on open wood fires, in preference to some oil stoves that had been provided, and a new dish called 'Wanstrow Pudding' was invented. Genuine work was carried out on the farms and the farmers were appreciative enough to ask them to stay longer but one senses that the weather got the better of them and they struck camp as planned, albeit 'on the wettest day of all'. The Scouts helped them on their return.

The numbers willing to participate seemed to be dwindling by 1945 and only 12 Weston pupils, who were joined by 18 boys from Yeovil Grammar School, went to Wanstrow. Again the weather wasn't very encouraging and three days of the two weeks were complete washouts. They had three ladies to help with the cooking. But spirits seemed buoyant, a concert was held, and although relatively muted, the news of the acceptance by the Japanese of the armistice terms was celebrated.

This trio of camps finished in 1946 with another return to Wanstrow. Numbers had increased to 16, supported by 10 boys from Cotham Grammar School. But not all was well it would seem. Farming in the area had moved away from cereal growing to increased grassland in order to step up milk and meat production, and thus there was less demand for labour. And, you guessed it , the weather was 'uniformly appalling all over England'. Only 6 days were worked out of a possible 11, as a result of which the Governments guaranteed minimum allowance had to be claimed to cover expenses. More recent recollection seems to suggest that two new members of the school staff had been dragooned into running this camp and they were not too pleased, and additionally, relationships with the Somerset War Agricultural Committee also seemed a bit tetchy.

And so the era of 'farming' camps, at least for the boys came to an end. The final act of these various camps came later in the year - we were paid. Well, sort of. As a Scout going to a Scout camp I never expected any cash reward and the money came as a pleasant surprise. Others had gone, more likely to the school's camps with at least some expectation of financial reward and when it came, some considered it derisory. A figure of about 25 shillings (£1.25) for the two weeks seems to stick in my mind. It was more the disposal of a small surplus than anything akin to an hourly rate.

My later and perhaps more mature recollection is that these camps took a lot more organising than we, as young boys, realised.

The Girls' Camps

The girl's camps before the final one at Pershore in 1946 do not appear to have been so well recorded, but they certainly occurred. Alison Day recalls going to a potato lifting harvest camp at Minsterworth, Gloucs in her 3rd or 4th form. The school was certainly there in 1943. Jean Innes recalls 'At one time I went on a school harvest camp to Finchampstead in Berkshire, and that I remember that myself, Thelma Owen and Anita Samuels sang in the fields, which were adjoining those of bandleader Jack Payne, in the vain hope of being 'discovered'. The girls at the harvest camp had to sleep in long dormitories. I had never shared a room with anyone, and these were still the days of innocence, so like most of us I dressed and undressed beneath the bedcovers. It was hard work in the fields, pulling turnips or potatoes. I can't remember which now, but I know it rained most of the time that we were there. After persuading my parents to let me go and that I would earn some money, I ended up with virtually nothing to show for it'.

The camp at Pershore, in Worcestershire, was the culmination of a series of four camps largely convened and organised by Miss White and Miss Moss. The previous three camps appear to have been at fixed sites but this one followed more on the lines of the Scout farming camps, with tented accommodation, largely erected by an advanced party of sixth formers who arrived 'a few days' ahead of the main party. Although under the guidance of the Worcestershire War Agricultural Committee, the contribution of that entity doesn't sound all that auspicious, and the advanced party had to contend with a confused pile of what turned out to be tents, bedding, straw, palliases, ground sheets and blankets. There were also some 'curious bits of iron' which turned out to be a cooking range and a boiler. However the view from the campsite 'was very beautiful'.

Whilst work on previous camps had been dominated by potato lifting, this time the work was mainly for market gardeners and fruit growers in the Pershore area, a role now largely met by itinerant and immigrant labour. The field work included black currant and raspberry picking, pea and leak hoeing, bean topping, picking and twining. This last job was apparently quite back breaking as the plants were kept to a height of 18 to 24 inches.

Some girls graded plums and others worked on a leak planting machine. Janet Lovell (Owen) remembers going to Pershore to actually lift potatoes and remembers working with Italian prisoners-of-war who 'used to make fires and roast potatoes - delicious! I still like roast potatoes!'- but we learn nothing long term about Italians. On the other hand, picking plums appears to have put her off plums, for life.

Seemingly, work was not always available so various excursions were made to Worcester, Evesham and Tewkesbury and to the local cinema - the 'Plaza'. Elizabeth Taylor in 'National Velvet' was showing. The Plaza had about ten seats per row and 'the audience conversed freely and audibly during the performance'. The weather seemed reasonably kind, gales and rain coming mainly at night. Girls joined in a local youth club social and put up a rounders team against a local side. It seems that the recollections of this camp were very positive and there does seem to have been an awareness that organising such camps was not simple.

At Pershore in 1946

But in 1946, the era of farming camps came to an end. Perhaps not so many from the two schools had taken part but those who did, seem to recall the events with a mixture of stoicism and enjoyment.

Additionally,

Aside from these quasi-formal school camps, Mr H. C. Wood took four senior 6th form boys to work in the forests in Scotland, in 1941. The work was very hard, mainly stripping felled trees of their bark for 3½d. a tree, later upp'd to 4d. However this meant that they were earning 6/- a day - considered at the time to be quite acceptable. The whole event was seemingly pursued under the benign patronage of the logging company (there seems to have been a friend of a friend dimension to the event) and they were allowed to keep their earnings. However what makes the account of this event so interesting is the journey there and back by train. Once again it accentuates the great difference in perception of distance and of travel, since those times. These days you could get to Australia more quickly and certainly with far less sense of adventure, than that war-time trip to Scotland.

ENTERTAINMENT, SOCIAL LIFE AND SUNDRIES

It must have been a case of 'what you don't know about, you don't miss', because any factual comparison of the 1940s with more modern times can but show the 1940s to have been pretty (very) dull and dreary. Yet people do not seem to remember it as such.

At home of course, it was the era of the radio only, with no television. There had been TV transmissions in the London area prior to the war but this ceased at the outbreak of hostilities. Radio had a dimension in people's lives that is difficult to conceive of, now. Some of the catch phrases of popular comedy shows, particularly ITMA ('Its That Man Again') such as 'can I do you now, Sir', 'after you Claude, no after you Cecil', 'its being so cheerful as keeps me going' and particularly 'TTFN' ('ta ta for now') which lasted for many years as a friendly farewell, became part of common day conversations. They would have been heard regularly at school.

The cinema was nearly all pervading. Weston had four cinemas at the beginning of the decade - the large and rather luxurious Odeon, the middle-of-the-road 'Regent', the 'Central' generally considered, perhaps unfairly, as a flea pit, and the 'Tivoli' which didn't seem to fit any particular description - a sort of centre of gravity of the other three. However, the 'Tivoli' in the Boulevard was burned down in the June 1942 air raids - and so that left three. Programmes tended to be continuous and thus the statement to one's companion that 'this is where we came in' was a commonplace observation. The Odeon had the marvellous Compton organ which emerged in ever changing colours, and 'it must be the interval because the organ is coming up' was another familiar comment. Taking a girl to the cinema for the first time was a major milestone in a schoolboy's path to maturity and deciding when, of if, to put your arm around the girl could seriously detract from one's concentration of what was going on, on the screen. I suppose the young lady then had the problem of whether to stay aloof or to mould into the cumbersome embrace, already challenged by the arm rest between them, and the ire, unless they were similarly engaged, of the people sitting behind. There were normally two feature films, an 'A' and a 'B', trailers for future films, the newsreel (an important component of wartime information and propaganda) and fixed frame advertisements. It was quite a comprehensive offering but at popular times you could queue for ages to get in, generally in lines headed by a board which carried the price of the seat that you were opting for. My antipathy towards queuing stems from that era.

On Saturday morning the Odeon at least, had a programme for children. Do I not recall that we use to sing,

> Every Saturday morning, where do we go?
> Getting into mischief, oh dear no!
> To the Mickey Mouse club, with our badges on,
> Every Saturday morning at the O-de-on!

Superb - nothing like it

At the outbreak of the war, BBC Light Entertainment moved to Bristol with a considerable overflow into Weston. The Winter Gardens and the Congregational Church Hall in the Boulevard became hosts to many of the national dance orchestras playing for the BBC's 'Band of the week' show. Frank Ashby recalls getting tickets for and listening to such illustrious bands of the time, as Harry Roy, Joe Loss, Eric Winston, Jack Payne and Oscar Rabin. This would have extended for older pupils, albeit a probable minority, to dances at the Winter Gardens on a Saturday evening. With the passing of time, many entered the ranks of the dancers at the Winter Gardens, which in that era were largely face-to-face and often cheek-to-cheek. Dances of one type only, came in threes, followed by a break during which time you planned your next move, with a particular gameplan for the last waltz. However with very rare exceptions these dances would have all terminated by midnight, with no drinks licence there at the time. If New Years Eve fell on a Saturday, the dance would still be over and the hall cleared by 11.45. For the more salubrious there was always the 'Knightstone Theatre' which afforded both professional and amateur performances of a wide range of offerings.

Social life in any corporate fashion was pretty thin in those days and would have been almost confined to Scouts, these visits to the cinema and the pretty minimal social content of away rugby games. There was, of course, no 'clubbing'. Nevertheless, boy/girl friendships were developing and for schoolgirls and schoolboys alike, the opposite sex became more and more a component of their thoughts and interests. Given the schools' segregation policy there was quite a big divide to bridge, but perhaps that was its own reward. It was fun bridging the gap. However, successes in even the most innocuous of carnal sense were few and far between and even at private Christmas parties which began to blossom in the post war years, 'Postman's knock', 'winking' 'Hyde

Park' and 'sardines' (details available on request) were about as exciting as these occasions got. In truth, 'sardines' could be played at the advanced level, and often was. Alcohol played virtually no part and any event that went on to near midnight was considered pretty mature. I suppose that we all had our private ambitions and fantasies but really these occasions, or this whole era, was grotesquely innocent. Yet I see I still have a number of letters from young ladies of that era with the stamps all askew, reflecting kisses and that old legend 'S.W.A.L.K' (sealed with a lover's kiss) on the reverse. In truth we did have our moments, but I'm not telling.

Even in that environment you did begin to learn that true love was not always smooth and that there was a thing called competition.

What is perhaps surprising is the large number of stable relationships, certainly of those who were at the Weston schools, that have survived from that era.

Of course for many younger pupils, toys were still a component of life although they became more difficult to acquire in the war years. At that age for boys, inviting friends to come around to 'play with their trains', was a consideration, as were the many board games that proliferated at that time. However, in general boys invited boys, and girls invited girls.

It was an era when you always felt safe. Even during the blackout days one could walk after dark as an individual and never feel threatened.

Other Activities.

Mainstream activities like school, homework and the closely associated Scouts or ATC didn't really fill the whole activities horizon, certainly not in the evenings or in the holidays. The ways of filling the surviving spaces reflected personal interests and seem largely unrecorded

In 1944, a new prize was presented to the school, in common with all other secondary schools in the County, by Mr. F. C. Tiarks. It was to be for the best essay on a subject connected with the British Empire. I think the pressure to participate was mainly moral, but I see that I spent a number of days in Weston's reference library writing an essay on Cecil Rhodes, during the Easter holiday in 1945. I didn't win. I doubt if the prize survived long into the era of the politically correct.

There were also other youth services in the town, such as the Sea Cadets and Army cadets - and in my case, in the 1942/44 period, it was the Red

Cross cadets. For others there was the St John's Ambulance junior section.

I believe that the St. John's cadets were occasionally involved in real events but the Red Cross seemed to be getting ready for events that never appeared to happen, or in which we were not involved. I cannot think now, why it appealed to me. We had a very simple 'uniform' - a white first aid , but in truth empty, linen bag strung across the body, a belt, and an armband. Not very sexy. We went to lectures and passed exams on first aid and home nursing. Indeed to this day I can still do a good blanket corner. We were often called to help with the collections at local cinemas in favour of the Red Cross and I can especially remember seeing, 'San Demetrio, London' a famous wartime epic about an oil tanker that just makes it to Malta at the height of the siege there, about half a dozen times in one week. We were also messengers at the local hospital's Casualty Department. I cannot recall anything more boring - nothing ever happened. Either real casualties went in through another door, or people didn't bother the hospitals as they do today. After several weeks, I just gave up. However as junior Red Cross members we did receive parcels from schoolchildren in the USA. These parcels had been individually assembled with small presents from American schoolchildren. In some measure it was rather strange to be recipients of such kindness, when we didn't feel that deprived. From the American standpoint however it must have seemed that children in the United Kingdom were going through a bad time. I fear that we took this gesture of kindness too readily and never thought of thanking anyone. Maybe it is not too late. Even at the time it seemed surprising that scarce shipping resources had been employed to get these parcels across the Atlantic.

Cycling was a core activity, both in company and on your own. I see that on Sunday, 15th April 1945, when still 14, I cycled to Cheddar, Wells, Glastonbury and back, a distance of about 51 miles, by myself. Frank Ashby cycled to Lyme Regis and back in one day in 1940 and in the absence of road signs found some of the route by the position of the sun. Gus Fletcher cycled to near Dulverton, Devon for a wartime holiday. Some of the senior boys among the evacuees used to cycle home for the longer holidays during the period that the threat to London seem to have subsided. This all intermingled with homework and school based activities, so I suppose that overall, we lead quite a full life.

On a somewhat different plane was the Outward Bound Sea School, at Aberdovey. In 1946 the County Education Committee decided to offer a number of bursaries to attend courses of four weeks duration at that school . The value of these bursaries, if I remember correctly, was fourteen guineas. The boys school - well they were only for boys of

course - but particularly the school Scouts, were leading applicants in the County for these bursaries and a number of us successfully applied for them. They were disciplined robust occasions, with a morning (very) cold shower at 06.30 to get the day underway and then seamanship, athletics, hill walking and some academic component to fill a very full day. There was also a three day voyage under sail, in Cardigan Bay. Earlier the school had been used to train ocean going mariners how to handle small boats in the event that they had to abandon ship as a result of enemy action. By 1946 the theme was training for life *through the sea,* not necessarily *for the sea.* They were good occasions, and those who went on them came back deservedly with a feeling of some achievement. Later on, the bursaries were extended to the Outward Bound Mountain School in the Lake District.

Outward Bound Sea School's ketch 'Garibaldi'.

Hardly a sundry, yet only one person has recalled the medical and dentist examinations that pupils underwent, at the school. They didn't appear to be on any regular basis and my own recollection errs towards the view that they slowly fizzled out. I do recall a doctor examined us, when I had just arrived in the third form from Mitcham school. He told me, on the basis of low blood pressure or slow pulse (or some such) that 'you ought to be a good athlete'. I am not quite sure that I ever proved to be so but I was carrying a fair measure of uncertainty at the time having just transferred from Mitcham and this was quite a fillip to my self assessment - in fact a whole new self-perception. Rugby suddenly seem to be more enjoyable and I started running a little harder - generally to reasonable effect.

The dentist came with his peddle driven drilling machine. He didn't have an assistant so he peddled and drilled at the same time, the whole contraption eventually folding away into his car at the end of the day. The only recollection that I have received, makes reference to the screams that came therefrom. I have a diary entry for 1945 which reads 'had front tooth stopped - awful'. Thank goodness things have improved since then.

The only other sundry that almost defies classification is 'Solomon' the goat. He belonged to a Mrs. Porcher but was moored in the girls tennis court enclosure - the only boy in the (girl's) school as Miss Farthing publicly acknowledged. His principal claim to notoriety was when he ate the groundsman's, Mr Evans' clothing coupons instead of his sweet ration, of which Solomon apparently new the whereabouts. Solomon had a penchant for paper and was sometimes fed old rough books by the girls - although I gather that this was at a page at a time and the staples were removed. There's compassion for you. Margaret England recalls that Solomon once slipped his tether and was looking into the classroom windows. Miss Brice was taking her carefully prepared lesson on Milton's 'Samson Agonistes'. This formidable teacher gradually became aware that she might have some opposition but she determined to finish the tense passage. Just as she reached the climax Solomon made some most strange noises which left the class convulsed. 'Mercy of Heaven, what hideous noise was this?' spluttered Miss Brice.

THE POST WAR YEARS

To the school girl and the school boy, the post war years didn't really present a world much different to the war years that preceded them. Of course there was no longer a threat of air raids but that threat had really disappeared in 1944. The blackout was lifted but public illumination was at a pretty modest level for years. The bulk of food rationing was maintained and the grey loaf prevailed. Indeed, as has been mentioned earlier, bread and cake rationing was introduced for the first time in 1946 with the advent of B.U's - bread units. Clothes rationing survived almost to the end of the decade. Foreign travel as a commonplace activity was all but non existent. Some of the most obvious improvements however were in things like the Outward Bound Sea School and the more imaginative Scout camps. The girls 'adopted' a school in Perigueux in the south-west of France and exchange visits were planned.

The principal changes were at a national political level, with the introduction by the Labour government elected in 1945, of the Health Service, and their nationalisation of the railways, the coal mines, and public utilities. To the average person the short term effect of all these was minimal. Even if big things were afoot, it made virtually no impact on pupils at school.

The re-emergence of national politics following the victory in Europe, bought a modest amount of political content to school life. Initially it was in the form, in the boys school at least, of a mock election in June 1945 to coincide with the national General Election. Procedures which mirrored the national event were rigorously enforced and three candidates were duly nominated, held meetings and sought votes. Boys from Form III upwards were the electorate. Come the declaration of the result, the Labour candidate had 77 votes, the Conservative 57, and the Liberal 55. By the end of the decade, there had been a swing to the right with the Conservative on 114, Labour with 72 and the Liberal 25. On that occasion, the Liberal candidate forfeited his deposit of 2/6d.

8th June, 1946

TO-DAY, AS WE CELEBRATE VICTORY, I send this personal message to you and all other boys and girls at school. For you have shared in the hardships and dangers of a total war and you have shared no less in the triumph of the Allied Nations.

I know you will always feel proud to belong to a country which was capable of such supreme effort; proud, too, of parents and elder brothers and sisters who by their courage, endurance and enterprise brought victory. May these qualities be yours as you grow up and join in the common effort to establish among the nations of the world unity and peace.

George R.I.

A message received by all school children from King George VI, commemorating the victory of World War 2.

What did effect us was the weather, particularly in 1947. From late January to March there were frequent and severe blizzards which caused the school to close every now and then, due to a combination of access problems and fuel shortage. For 12th February my diary carried a hopeful possibility - 'no exams?' Later that week I wrote "England's position seems pretty grim. Black out, no fuel; only want the sirens [to be like the war]. Poor Mr Shinwell [the Labour Minister of 'Fuel and Power']". For the 6th March my diary reads 'No school because of blizzard the previous night. Snow thicker than before', an almost Dickensian image.

The school 1945-46 rugby team. Very much a 'shortly after the war' photo. The team pose in front of the blast wall built in 1943 outside the gymnasium, and only five team members have surviving school rugby shirts - a reflection of those times.

Later that week I wrote 'Apparently this week's blizzard was the worst in recorded history'. It wasn't all bad news. The freed up hours were spent tobogganing down Uphill hill with any surviving segregation policy, in tatters.

Of course, overall, things *were* improving with more school visits, the scout camps became more imaginative, and slowly the girls began to re-occupy their rebuilt classrooms. But sadly there was still time for some to pay the ultimate price. David Clothier who was in the fifth form in 1945 and was a colleague of many who come to the school reunion, was killed in action with the Somerset Light Infantry in Malaya, early in the 1950s.'

But the great educational changes, in content, attitude and discipline, were yet to come and at school, the 1940s continued to retain a sameness - indeed a continuity - right through to the end of the decade.

AND FINALLY

In 1995, Gordon Lawrence had the initiative of convening a reunion of those boys who had taken their School Certificate in 1945, that is, a reunion after a lapse of 50 years. About 60 past pupils would have been eligible. On the day, 31 past pupils were present, 8 sent apologies, 4 were overseas and alas, 8 were dead, leaving about 10 unaccounted for. This was a remarkable acheivement after such a long passage of time.

The reunion was held at the school, with lunch at a local hotel, and deemed a great success. It immediately migrated to an annual event.

In 1998, Alison Finney organised a similar event for the girls and soon afterwards the boys and girls events were amalgamated and the franchise extended to anyone who had been at the school at least 50 years before. The event is now well established as an annual event and the most recent in 2004 saw about 140 sitting down to lunch at the Royal Hotel, in Weston. The spirit of the forties was very alive and well.

So how do you sum it all up?

I think that I have to chicken out and take advantage of someone else's recollections that they have been kind enough to record for me.

Gus Fletcher, by his own admissions seems to have been a bit wayward at school, an occasional absolute idiot he admits, and caned for smoking at one time. This attitude to the world took him to the Palestine Police and when that was disbanded, to the Malayan Police in an intelligence driven fight against the Chinese insurgents. He learned Cantonese Chinese and followed by an intensive two year post graduate course at Cambridge University in Mandarin. He eventually became a Political Counsellor at the British Embassy in New Delhi but retains an 'inextricable link to China' and is retained as a 'China watcher', by interested agencies.

Gus is most fulsome in his praise for the school. 'What a marvellous school it was, what wonderful friends we made', he has recorded. 'The way that the school carried on in the vicissitudes of war was remarkable' He has expressed 'amazement at the standards achieved by dedicated teachers and a pretty firm discipline'.

I'll settle for that.

THE 'SCHOLARSHIP' PAPERS - 1941

County Examination for the Award of Special Places, held on Friday, 7th March 1941

1. ARITHMETIC (Written)   (9.50 a.m. - 11.25 a.m.)

2. ENGLISH COMPOSITION   (11.40 a.m. - 12.15 a.m.)
   (FIRST EXERCISE)

3. ENGLISH COMPOSITION   (1.30 p.m. - 2.35 p.m.)
   (SECOND EXERCISE)

4. GENERAL ENGLISH PAPER   (2.40 p.m. - 4.10 p.m.)

Before the written Arithmetic paper there was a mental arithmetic test

Somerset County Council.

THE COUNTY EDUCATION COMMITTEE
County Examination for the Award Of Special Places, 1941.

ARITHMETIC (Written)
(9.50 a.m.-11.25 a.m.)

You should answer all the questions if you, can.

1. Multiply seventeen thousand eight hundred and sixty-five by a number which is eleven less than fifty.

2 A club had £189 12s. 6d. for the Christmas share-out. There were 74 members. How much did each member receive?

3. New black-out blinds are needed for thirteen windows in a house. Six blinds must be 1yd. 3 inches long and seven must be 1 yd. 9 inches. What length of material is required ? Allow *2* inches of material on each blind for turning in.

4. At a canteen one day, the takings are as follows: 3 £1 notes, 5 10/- notes, 13 half-crowns, 21 florins 15 shillings, 44 sixpences and 21 pennies. What is the total amount?

5. A tank which holds 1,000 gallons weighs, when empty, 3 cwt. 3 qrs. What is the weight of the tank and its contents when it is full of water ? Note: A pint of water weighs a pound and a quarter.

6. A shopman stated that I could buy a wireless set for cash for £8 19s. 6d., or that I could have the same set by payment of £1, the remainder to be paid in eleven monthly instalments of 17s. 6d. each. How rnuch do I save by paying cash?

7 On the shortest day the sun rises at 8.2 a.m. and sets at 3.53 p.m. On the longest day it rises at 3.42 a.m. and sets at 8.21 p.m. How much longer is the sun above the horizon on the longest dav than on the shortest.?

8.. A garden plot 50 feet by 30 feet is to be planted with cabbages. They are to be set 2 feet apart in the row and 2 feet between the rows ; the outside, plants in both directions are one foot from the edges of the plot.Draw this plot, marking one row of cabbages down the short side.

How rnanv cabbages can you plant in the whole plot ?

Somerset County Council.

THE COUNTY EDUCATION COMMITTEE
County Examination for the Award of Special Places, 1941.

ENGLISH COMPOSITION-FIRST EXERCISE
(11.40 a.m.-12.15 p.m.)

Write a composition of **not less than thirty lines** on **one only**
of the following-

1. A pet animal and how to look after it.

2. Your favourite magazine or weekly paper and why you like to read it.

3. Someone has written promising you a fortnight's holiday in the summer and asks where you would like to go and what you would like to do and see. Write a suitable letter in reply.

4. The story of *either*

(a) Cinderella;
 or
(b) The Pied Piper;
 or
(c) William Tell
 or
(d) Robinson Crusoe.

Somerset County Council.

THE COUNTY EDUCATION COMMITTEE
County Examination for the Award of Special Places, 1941.

ENGLISH COMPOSITION-SECOND EXERCISE
(1.30 p.m.-2.35 p.m.)

You will have ten minutes in which to read this passage slowly and carefully, and then you will be given a set of questions to answer upon it. You will be allowed to keep this paper before you while you answer the questions.

THE OLD DOG

Caesar was an old valued dog, although of no superior breed; he was just an ordinary dog of the country, shorthaired, with long legs and a blunt muzzle. Usually the native dog was about the size of a Scotch collie; Caesar was quite a third larger and it was said of him that he was as much above all other dogs of the house in intelligence and courage as in size. He was a black dog, now in his old age sprinkled with white hairs all over his body, the face and legs having gone quite grey. Caesar in a rage, or on guard at night, or when driving cattle in from the plains, was a terrible being; with us children he was mild-tempered and patient, allowing us to ride on his back.

Now in his decline he grew irritable and surly and ceased to be our playrnate. The last two or three months of his life were very sad and it troubled us to see him so gaunt, with his big ribs clearly visible on his sides, and to watch his twitchings when he dozed. We noticed, too, how painfully he struggled to get up on his feet and we wanted to know why this was so and why we could not give him something to make him well. For answer they would open his great mouth to show us his teeth - the big blunt canines and old molars worn down to stumps. Old age was what ailed him; he was thirteen years old.

Somerset County Council.

THE COUNTY EDUCATION COMMITTEE
County Examination for the Award of Special Places, 1941.

ENGLISH COMPOSITION-SECOND EXERCISE
(1.40 p.m.-2.35 p.m.)

Answer all the following questions if you can, using your own words. Make your answers clear but short.

1. (a.)
   What do you learn from the passage about the native dogs of the country ?

   (b) How did Caesar differ from them ?

2. What was Caesar's work ?

3. What change was there in Caesar's character as he approached his end ?

4. How did the children know the dog was ill ?

5. How did they learn what ailed him?

6. What is there in the passage to make you think the author did not live in Great Britain when a child?

7. What do you understand by the following words and phrases :

   clearly visible, sprinkled with, irritable, gaunt, it troubled us ?

Somerset County Council.
THE COUNTY EDUCATION COMMITTEE
County Examination for the Award of Special Places, 1941.

GENERAL ENGLISH PAPER
(2.40 p.m.-4.10 p.m.)

SECTION A

(You should answer all the questions in this section if you can.)

1. What single words can be used instead of the following expressions -
At once, in haste, at last, with success, in the direction of ?

2. People who write books are called authors. What do we call-

    People who do not tell the truth;
    People who betray their country ;
    People who are very holy;
    People who are very brave;
    People who copy other people ?

3. Copy down this table and fill in the blank spaces.

Present Tense	past Tense
I laugh	I laughed
I see	-
I draw	-
I have	-
1 hear	-
1 lose	-
I grow	-
I sing	-
I catch	-
I bring	-
I fetch	-

4. Write out the first verse of the National Anthem.

5. Here are three pairs of words. For each pair write one sentence which will show that you understand the difference in meaning between the two words.

    (a) take, snatch; (b) write, scribble; (c) look, stare.

SECTION B

*Answer only **two** of the following questions*

1. Copy the following table and complete it.

country	Inhabitants
England	The English
Norway	-
Sweden	-
Spain	-
Canada	-
Greece	-
Poland	-
France	-
Japan	-
New Zealand	-
Holland	-

2 Which of the following people lived first ?
    (1) William Shakespeare or William Caxton.
    (2) George Washington or Sir Francis Drake.
    (3) Archbishop Becket or St. Augustine of Canterbury.

    Give reasons for your answer in each case.

3. In this diagram B stands for Birmingham, the lines for main roads and the numbers for the towns they lead to -viz.,
Bristol, Cardiff, Carlisle, Holyhead, Hull, London, Liverpool, Newcastle-on-Tyne, Norwich and Southampton.

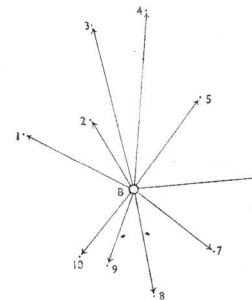

Write down the numbers in a column and against each number write the name of the place you think the number stands for.

APPENDIX TWO

PAPERS FOR THE OXFORD LOCAL EXAMINATIONS - 1941
(THE OXFORD SCHOOL CERTIFICATE)

OSC NUMBER	SUBJECT	DATE OF EXAMINATION	PAGE NUMBER
S1	ENGLISH LANGUAGE	July 16th	1
S2	SHAKESPEARE &c.	July 14th	2
S7	ENGLISH HISTORY (1815-1919)	July 15th	7
S15(a)	GEOGRAPHY I	July 10th	8
S15(b)	GEOGRAPHY II	July 10th	8
S18(a)	FRENCH I	July 11th	9
S18(b)	FRENCH II	July 11th	10
S23	ARITHMETIC	July 16th	11
S24	GEOMETRY	July 15th	12
S25	ALGEBRA	July 18th	13
S26	TRIGONOMETRY	July 22nd	14
S32	THEORETICAL CHEMISTRY	July 14th	15
S35	PRACTICAL CHEMISTRY	July 9th	16
S37(a)	PHYSICS I	July 11th	16
S37(b)	PHYSICS II	July 17th	18

There were of course papers in many other subjects but these are the ones taken by Ray Millard in 1941
To improve the legibility and to make them more compact these papers have been reformatted.

OXFORD LOCAL EXAMINATIONS
SCHOOL CERTIFICATE
WEDNESDAY, JULY 16, 1941
TIME ALLOWED-2 Hours
English Language

[**Special attention must be paid to the construction of
sentences, as well as to spelling and punctuation.**]
ALL questions should be attempted.

One hour should be sufficient for Question 5.

1. Construct eight sentences (one for each word) to show clearly that
you understand the meanings of four of the following pairs of words
(a) *lain, laid; (b) elder, older; (c) displace, replace; (d) elicit, illicit; (e)
sensible, sensitive; (f) repair,impair*

2. Write a clear and concise summary, in readable form, giving the
substance of lines 11-30 (from 'He did not stand' to the end) of the
following passage (your summary should not exceed one-third of the
original in length; the original passage contains about 180 words in
lines 11-30):-

We had on board a follow-passenger whose discourse in verity
might have beguiled a longer voyage than we meditated. He was a dark,
Spanish-complexioned young man, with an officer-like assurance and
an insuppressible volubility of assertion. He was, in fact, the greatest
liar I had met with then, or since. He was none of your hesitating, half
story-tellers (a most painful description of mortals) who go on sounding
your belief, and only giving you as much as they see you can swallow at
a time, but one who committed daylight depredations upon his
neighbour's faith. He did not stand shivering on the brink, but was a
hearty, thorough-paced liar and plunged at once into the depths of your
credulity. Not many rich, not many wise, or learned, composed at that
time the common stowage of a Margate packet. We were, I am afraid, a
set of unseasoned Londoners - let our enemies give it a worse name.
There might be an exception or two among us, but I scorn to make any
invidious distinctions among such a jolly, companionable ship's
company as those were whom I sailed with.
   Had the confident fellow told us half the legends on land which he
favoured us with on the other element, I flatter myself the good sense of
most of us would have revolted. But we were in a new world, with
everything unfamiliar about us, and the time and place disposed us to
the reception of any prodigious marvel whatsoever. Time has
obliterated from my memory much of his wild fablings; and the rest
would appear dull, as written and to be read on shore.

(From CHARLES LAMB's *The Old Margate Hoy.*)

3. Analyse into clauses lines 1-6 of the passage printed in Question 2
- (from 'We had on board' to 'then, or since').

(Example: *When he saw that no advantage was to be gained by
advancing, he halted.*
When ... Saw   Adverb clause qualifying 'halted'.
that ... Advancing   Noun clause, object of 'saw'.
he halted   Main clause.
You may use the terms to which you are accustomed.)

4. Answer **briefly** the following questions in regard to the
passage printed in Question 2:-
   (a) Give the meaning of the following phrases:(i) an
officer-like assurance; (ii) the depths of your credulity; (iii)
invidious distinctions.
   (b) Give **three** examples of metaphorical expression in the
passage.
   (c) What is a parenthesis? Give **two** examples from the
printed passage.
   (d) Point out **three** words or phrases in the passage which
appear to you to be unusual or to be employed in an unusual way.
   (e) 'Time has obliterated from my memory much of his wild
fablings' (lines 28-9). Point out in what respects this sentence is
more effective than if Lamb had written. 'I have forgotten many
of his stories'.

5. Write a composition on any one of the following topics:-
   [Remember that regard will be paid chiefly to soundness of
   style and suitability of material, and not to mere length. A
   good composition of a page and a half, in handwriting of
   average size, will be sufficient to earn a high mark, and your
   composition must not exceed three pages in length.]
   (a) Wild life in the woods.
   (b) Looking forward.
   (c) The effect of the war on your school.
   (d) A local 'character'.
   (e) This machine age.

OXFORD LOCAL EXAMINATIONS
SCHOOL CERTIFICATE
MONDAY, JULY 14, 1941
TIME ALLOWED 2 Hours.
Shakespeare, &C.

[You must attempt Section A, and EITHER Section B OR Section C-two Sections in all. In Section A answer the first question which is set on your Shakespeare play, and TWO of the other three questions on that play - three questions in all on Shakespeare. If you are offering Section B, answer the two questions on your book of poetry, or else, if you are offering Section C, answer the two on your book of prose.

Your answers must be given up in two separate batches, corresponding to the two Sections. Remember therefore not to answer any part of a question from one Section on the same page of your answers as a question from the other Section.

On each page of your answers to Section A write SHAKESPEARE in the space allowed for Name of Examination Paper; for Section B write POETRY; for Section C write PROSE. Number the pages in each Section 1, 2, &c.

The questions marked with an asterisk (*) should be answered as fully as time allows.]

SECTION A   SHAKESPEARE

The Tempest

A 1. Choose two of the following extracts, and answer **very briefly** the questions below each of the extracts you choose:

>   In the deep nook, where once
>   Thou called'st me up at midnight to fetch dew
>   From the still-vex'd Bermoothes; there she's hid.

(i) Who speaks these words, and to whom ? To what does 'she' (in the last line) refer?
(ii) Explain the phrase, 'the still-vex'd Bermoothes'.
(iii) Why should this phrase be of especial interest to the audience of Shakespeare's time ?

>   Thou liest, thou jesting monkey thou;
>   I would my valiant master would destroy thee:
>   I do not lie.

(i) Who speaks these words, and to whom? To whom does he refer as 'my valiant master'?
(ii) What causes him to say, 'Thou liest'?
(iii)In the same scene occurs a speech beginning, 'Be not afeard: the isle is full of noises'.
Quote the next **two and a half** lines.

c)
>   I'll break my staff,
>   Bury it certain fathoms in the earth,
>   And, deeper than did ever plummet sound,
>   I'll drown my book.

(i) What happens immediately after these words are spoken ?
(ii) Who speaks these words? For what did he use his staff and book?
(iii) What does he require before he breaks his staff, and for what purpose does he require it?

2. Summarize Ferdinand's experiences as narrated and represented in this play, and add a sketch of his character.
*A3. Give a brief account of the last seen in *The Tempest*, and show how it provides a happy ending.
*A 4. 'Like the masques that were becoming so popular, The *Tempest* provides much to please the eye and ear.' Show what The *Tempest* provides in these respects.

SECTION A. SHAKESPEARE

Henry the Fourth (Part II)

A 5. Choose two of the following extracts, and answer **very briefly** the questions below each of the extracts you choose:

(a)
>   0 thou fond many! with what loud applause
>   Didst thou beat heaven with blessing Bolingbroke
>   Before he was what thou wouldst have him be.

(i) Explain the phrase, 'fond many'. Who was Bolingbroke ? Explain the last line of the extract.
(ii) Who speaks these words, and in whose presence ?
(iii) Quote the two lines preceding this extract which comment on the instability of popular favour.

(b)   Thy wish was father, Harry, to that thought.

(i) To what thought does the speaker refer ? What does he mean by saying that Harry's wish was father to it ? What had Harry just done ?
(ii) State briefly the explanation that Harry offers of his action.
(iii) How does this explanation affect our opinion of his character ?

(c)   What! rate, rebuke, and roughly send to prison
        The immediate heir of England? Was this easy?
        May this be wash'd in Lethe, and forgotten?

(i) Who speaks these words, and to whom, and on what occasion ?
(ii) To what incident is he referring?
(iii) Explain the phrase, 'May this be wash'd in Lethe ?

*A 6. Describe briefly Falstaff's two visits to Shallow, and include summaries of Falstaff's soliloquies on these occasions. What light is thrown on Shallow's character in these scenes ?

*A 7. Describe the character of (i) King Henry IV,and (ii) Pistol, showing carefully from what passages in the play you draw your evidence.

*A 8. Which of the following words best describes what you feel about Falstaff in this play - admiration, amusement, contempt, or sympathy ? Give full reasons for your choice, based on details of the play.

SECTION A. SHAKESPEARE

Romeo and Juliet

A 9. Choose two of the following extracts, and answer **very briefly** the questions below each of the extracts you choose:

(a)   And in this state she gallops night by night
        Through lovers' brains, and then they dream of love.

(i) Quote any **three** consecutive lines describing the chariot or the equipment with which this gallop is undertaken.
(ii) Whose chariot is it? Who describes it?
(iii) Mention two other kinds of persons whose dreams are described in this speech, and what they are said to dream about.

(b)   No, tis riot so deep as a well, nor so wide as a church door;
        but 'tis enough, 'twillserve: ask for me to-morrow, and you shall
        find me a grave man.

(i) Who speaks these words?, What is it that is'not so deep as a well', and who had given it to him ?
(ii) What is characteristic of the speaker ill the last sentence of this extract ?
(iii) One well-known actor used to arrange the play so that this character died on the stage. Whv was this a mistake ?

(c)   As I remember, this should be the house:
        Being holiday, the beggar's shop is shut.

(i) Mention any **three** details of the equipment of this shop.
(ii) What does Romeo want to buy, and why?
(iii) What sort of a shop is it ? Why does Shakespeare arrange for it to be shut ?

*A 10. Sketch the character of Romeo, indicating carefully on what evidence your sketch is based. Add a brief discussion of the question whether he is to be regarded as himself responsible for his misfortunes, or as the victim of fate.
*A 11. Give an account of the scene iln which Romeo in the orchard talks to Juliet at her window. Point out the especial beauties of this scene.
*A 12. Sketch the character of (i) Juliet's Nurse, and (ii) Juliet's father. Show in what ways they add interest to the play.

SECTION B. POETRY

CHAUCER: *The Prologue, 11. 1-714*

B 1. Choose **two** of the following extracts, and answer **very briefly** the questions below each of the extracts you choose:

(a)   Of fustian he wered a gipoun
        Al bismotored with his habergeoun.

(i) Explain the words, 'fustian', 'gipoun', and 'habergeoun'.
(ii) What excuse is given for this pilgrim being in this condition ?
(iii) To which pilgrim do these lines refer? What are we told about his horse ?

(b)   To liven in delyt was ever his wone,
              For he was Epicurus owne sone.

(i) To whom do these lines refer? Why does Chaucer call him 'Epicurus owne sone'?
(ii) Quote (or give the substance of) any two lines describing how his house was provisioned.
(iii) Mention any two offices or positions that he had held, and explain what they were.

(c)   And thus, with feyned flaterye and japes,
            He made the person and the peple his apes.

(i) To whom do these lines refer? Mention **two** things that he possessed which he declared to be valuable treasures.
(ii) What song did he sing? What sort of a voice had he ?
(iii) Who rode with him on the pilgrimage? What was the official duty of this companion of his ?

*B 2. **Either,** (a) Show, from Chaucer's descriptions of the pilgrims, how accurately he observed costume and equipment.

    Or, (b) If you had been one of the company, which of the pilgrims would you have best liked to ride with as your chief companion, and which would you have most wished to avoid? Give full reasons from the impressions that you have gained of them from Chaucer.

SECTION B. POETRY
BYRON: *Selections* (ed. Walmsley), pp.

1-157

B 3. Choose **two** of the following extracts, and answer **very briefly** the questions below each of the extracts you choose:

(a)   And all went merry as a marriage-bell;
           But hush! hark! a deep sound strikes
             like a rising knell!

(i) The stanza from which these lines are taken begins
      'There was a sound of revelry by night.'
Quote the next **three** lines.

(ii) What was the deep sound that struck like a rising knell? Who was the first to hear it?
(iii) What important event occurred on the day after this revelry, and what other important event two days after that?

(b)   'England! with all thy faults 1 love thee still,'
          I said at Calais, and have not forgot it;
          I like to speak and lucubrate my fill;
           I like the government (but that is not it);
          I like the freedom of the press and quill;
          I like the Habeas Corpus (when we've got it).

(i) Name the poem from which these lines are taken. Does the first line of the extract lead you to expect lines like those that follow ? Give reasons for your opinion.
(ii) What do you think of the rhyming in this extract ?
(iii) What was the Habeas Corpus?

(c)   The mountains look on Marathon
        And Marathon looks on the sea;
        And rousing there an hour alone,
         I dream'd that Greece might still be free.

(i) Why did Byron dream of freedom for Greece at Marathon? Quote the two lines following this extract.
(ii) Name two other famous battles mentioned in this poem.
(iii) Give in your own words two examples from this poem of what Byron felt about the Greeks off his own time.

*B 4. **Either,** (a) Give an account of two of the following passages, and point out what is attractive in each of the two that you choose:-(i) *In Spain; (ii) Rome,* and *The Coliseum; (iii)* the extract from *Manfred; (iv) George III at St. Peter's Gate; (v) Newstead Abbey* (from *Don Juan).*

    Or, (b) What impression of Byron himself have you gained irom reading these Selections? Show from what passages your impression is derived.

SECTION B. POETRY
TENNYSON: *Selections* (King's Treasuries)

B 5. Choose **two** of the following extracts, and answer **very briefly** the questions below each of the extracts you choose:

(a)
> I chatter over stony ways,
> In little sharps and trebles,
> I bubble into eddying bays,
> I babble on the pebbles.

(i) Give the title of the poem in which this stanza occurs. Why are stanzas like this interspersed at various points in the poem?
(ii) What is especially noticeable about the sound of these lines ? What is such a device called?
(iii) What good deed does the supposed teller of the story in this poem represent himself as having done ?

(b)
> Far below them roars
> The long brook falling thro' the clov'n ravine
> In cataract after cataract to the sea.

(i) These lines occur in Œ*none*. Name the three goddesses who are the central figures in her story.
(ii) Why do they meet Paris ?
(iii) Point out any **two** respects in which this extract is an improvement on the following description of the stream in an earlier version of Œ*none:-*

> 'The loud glen river, which hath worn
> A path thro' steep-down granite walls below.'

c)
> Juts of slippery crag that rang
> Sharp-smitten with the dint of armed heels-
> And on a sudden, lo! the level lake,
> And the long glories of the winter moon.

(i) From what poem are these lines taken ? To whose 'armed heels' do they refer ? What does he see when he reaches the lake ?
(ii) By comparing the last two lines of this extract with the first two, point out what skilful use of sound effects is noticeable in these four lines.

*B 6. Either, *(a) Geraint and Enid* and *Enoch Arden* are the two longest poems in these Selections. Do you think that they are the most attractive poems in the book ? Give full reasons for your opinion, referring both to the subject matter and to the poetic expression of these and other poems.

Or, (b) Illustrate from these Selections Tennyson's admiration of fine character, pointing out some of the qualities that he especially admires.

SECTION C. PROSE

BUNYAN: *Pilgrim.s Progress, Part I*

1

C 1. Choose two of the following extracts, and answer **very briefly** the questions below each of the extracts you choose:

(a) Just as they had ended this talk, they drew near to a very miry slough, that was in the midst of the plain, and they being heedless, did both fall suddenly into the bog.

(i) Who was Christian's companion at this point? What other companion had they previously had? What was the slough called?
(ii) Why did Christian begin to sink in it? Who helped him out?
(iii) Explain the allegorical meaning of this slough.

(b) So when I came to myself again. I cried him mercy; but he said, I know not how to show mercy, and with that knockt me down again.

(i) Faithful speaks these words. Who was it who knocked him down, and what reason did he give for knocking him down the first time? Who stopped him from making an end of Faithful?
(ii) What is the allegorical significance of being knocked down repeatedly by this man?
(iii) How and where did Faithful die?

(c) There were also of them that had wings, and they answered one another without intermission, saying,-- -- -- -- -- -- And after that, they shut up the gates: which when I had seen, I wished myself among them.

(i) Quote the six words that should fill the blanks here.

(ii) What book is Bunyan recalling in the first half of this extract, and what particular part of it ?

(iii) What happens to Ignorance in the closing paragraph of this book immediately following this extract ?

*C 2. **Either,** (a) Describe Christian's experiences in any two of the following:-The Valley of Humiliation; Doubting Castle; The Delectable Mountains. State briefly the allegorical significance of the two passages that you have described.

Or, (b) 'In *Pilgrim's Progress* Bunyan intersperses among imaginative scenes recollections of things seen and heard in English life.' Illustrate the truth of this remark

SECTION C. PROSE

STEVENSON: An Inland Voyage

Choose **two** of the following extracts, and answer **very briefly** the questions below each of the extracts you choose:

(a)Might not this have been a brave African traveller, or gone to the Indies after Drake? But it is an evil age for the gypsily inclined among men. He who can sit squarest on a three-legged stool, he it is who has the wealth and glory.

(i) This is Stevenson's comment on a man who complained to him of the monotony of his occupation. What was his occupation, and in what town?

(ii) What African traveller might Stevenson have named? Suggest a reason why he does not name him although he names Drake.

(iii) Point out **two** respects in which the last sentence of this extract is more effective than if Stevenson had written, ' The man who works in an office gets money and becomes famous'.

(b) 'Listen, listen,'he said, bearing on the boy's shoulder, 'and remember this, my son.' A little after he went out into the garden suddenly, and I could hear him sobbing in the darkness.

(i) Where did this man come from ? What did he want his son to remember ?

(ii) Why was the man so moved by this?

(iii) What **two** details make the picture of the man's distress so vivid?

(c) A camp of conical white tents without the town looked like a leaf out of a picture Bible; sword-belts decorated the walls of the cafes, and the streets kept sounding all day long with military music. It was not possible to be an Englishman and avoid a feeling of elation.

(i) What book in the Bible might have an illustration picturing a camp of tents, and why? Why did Stevenson as an Englishman feel elated while he watched the French soldiers ?

(ii) In the next few lines he gives a picture of Highlanders marching. Mention any two details of this picture.

(iii) This camp was at Compiegne. What **two** features of the town hall there does Stevenson describe in detail?

C4. **Either,** (a) Give an account of Stevenson's experiences at any two of the places which he visited in his *Inland Voyage,* and his comments in connexion therewith. Add some lines on Stevenson's character as revealed in the two sections of which you have treated.

Or, (b) 'What a charming companion Stevenson must have been on a holiday!' Illustrate from *An Inland Voyage* the truth of this comment.

SECTION C. PROSE

Prose of Our Time (ed. Ratcliff), pp. 1-229

C 5. Choose **two** of the following extracts, and answer **very briefly** the questions below each of the extracts you choose:

(a) A gust of curiosity stirred the assembled guests. The apparition. from a world so different from theirs of this huge bent old man, pipe-smoking and tweed-jacketed, seemed strangely portentous.

(i) Who wrote this? Who was this old man, and why was he dressed like this?

(ii) Where was he at this moment? What had. drawn him there?

(iii) Why is the first sentence of this extract more effective than if the author had written, 'The assembled guests felt curious'?

(b) The architect whose design was selected, both by the committee and by the Queen, was Mr. Gilbert Scott, whose industry, conscientiousness, and genuine piety had brought him to the head of his profession.

i) What style did this architect favour ? For what work was his design now selected? Name the Queen.

(ii) What is there in this extract that is ironical?

(iii) Who wrote it? Mention one other example of his irony.

(c) The vividest poetry is that which sets itself like music, generation after generation, to the acts of life, as even Nero died with Homer on his lips, or Taillefer rode chanting the song of Roland up Senlac Hill, or Wolfe passed up the darkness of the St. Lawrence to his last battle, repeating the *Elegy* of Gray.

(i) What position did Nero hold? Where is Senlac Hill? Name Wolfe's last battle.
(ii) What is notable about the arrangement and structure of the last part of this extract (from 'as even Nero...')?
(iii) Under what ruler does the author of this extract think that Athens showed 'an active, many-sided beauty of daily life'? And what English writer of the Victorian age does he praise for the same virtue?

*C 6. **Either,** (a) Name the **three** pieces which you have most enjoyed in *Prose of Our Time,* and show fully what qualities in them account for your enjoyment. Then state which of the three you like best, and show why you prefer it to the other two.

Or, (b) Modern writers are sometimes accused of being too obscure or fanciful or difficult. Would you bring such charges against any writers represented in this book? Would you wholly acquit any of them of such charges ? Refer to the book in detail to justify your answer.

OXFORD LOCAL EXAMINATIONS
SCHOOL CERTIFICATE
TUESDAY, JULY 15, 1941
TIME ALLOWED - 2 ¼. Hours
English History, 1815-1919

[Write **ENGLISH HISTORY D** at the head of each sheet of your answers.
Answer **FIVE** questions. Credit will be given for SIMPLE sketch-maps whenever they are appropriate.]

1. Give some account of the personality and aims of three of the following -William Cobbett, Francis Place, the Earl of Durham, Jeremy Bentham, Robert Owen.
2. Give an account of the foreign policy of Canning.
3. What were the grievances of the Roman Catholic Church in Ireland in this period? When and how were they remedied?
4. Give short accounts of **two** of the following:

(a) the Australian gold discoveries and their results, *(b)* the causes of the Indian Mutiny, (c) the relations of Great Britain with Egypt, (d) responsible government in the British Empire.
5. What reforms do you connect with the name of Sir Robert Peel
6.Describe either (a) the growth and decline of the Chartist Movement, or *(b)* the development of Trade Unions.
7. Choose two Victorian leaders of thought in religion, science, or art, and describe the work and influence of each.
8. Give the chief provisions of the Second and Third Reform Acts, and explain how each Act came to be passed.
9. Give an account of the chief social reforms of the Liberal Governments of 1906 to 1914.
10. For what reasons and in what circumstances did Britain come to a friendly understanding with (a) France, (b)Russia in the early years of this century ?
11. **Either**, (a) Give a general account of the causes of friction in Europe created by the Peace of Versailles.

Or, (b) Describe the progress of the social services in Great Britain from, 1919 to 1933.

OXFORD LOCAL EXAMINATIONS
SCHOOL CERTIFICATE
THURSDAY, JULY 10, 1941
TIME ALLOWED-1½ Hours
Geography. I
General and World Geography

**[Write GEOGRAPHY 1 at the head of each sheet of your answers.
Answer Questions 1 and 2 and ONE other.
Credit will be given for appropriate sketch-maps; but
Candidates should not make them too elaborate..
Both Maps (A and B) must be given up with your answers.]**

1. Examine map A
(a) Write a description of the valley of the River Severn.
(b)Mark with an arrow at the point X at the bottom of the map the direction in which the river is flowing. The map must be given up.
(c) Write notes on the position of Welshpool (D.2). Compare it with Guilsfield (B.1). What reasons does the map suggest for the growth of Welshpool to be the more important of the two?
(d) Describe and explain the distribution of woodland on the map.

2.On the accompanying map of the world, B
(a) Name the two ocean currents marked by arrows.

(b) Name the four mountain-ranges marked A.

(c) Name the four groups of islands marked B.

(d) Write, on the margin of the map, the type of
natural vegetation found in the three shaded areas marked C.

(e) Which of the three areas marked D has the highest and which
the lowest mean annual rainfall?
Mark the highest 1 and the lowest 3.

3. Refer to Map A.

What are consequent rivers ? On Map A the Severn is a
consequent river. Mark **two** others with the letters
CON, and write the square references in the margin.
Write notes on the drainage of Long Mountain.

4. Refer to Map A.

Show how physical features have affected the distribution of human
settlement in the area shown on the map.

5. Refer to Map B.

The map shows the January isotherm of 32° F. in the Northern
Hemisphere and the July isotherm of 32° F. in the Southern
Hemisphere. Explain carefully why one is nearly parallel to lines
of latitude and the
other departs widely from them.

6. Refer to Map B.

The three areas marked X are regions of small population. Explain
why this is so. Note any marked differences between the regions.

OXFORD LOCAL EXAMINATIONS
SCHOOL CERTIFICATE
THURSDAY, JULY 10, 1941
TIME ALLOWED-1½ Hours

Geography. II
Regional Geography

**[Write GEOGRAPHY 11 at the head of each sheet of your answers.
Answer THREE questions, at least ONE from each of the Sections
A and B. The third question may be chosen from either Section A
or Section B.
Credit will be given for appropriate sketch-maps; but Candidates
should not make them too elaborate.]**

SECTION A

The following figures give density of population per square mile.
Suggest reasons for the density in each area:

Highlands of Scotland	less than 50
East Anglia	250
Glamorganshire	over 500.

2. Show how geographical factors have affected railway and road
communications in the British Isles between lines joining the Mersey
and Humber and the Forth and Clyde.

3. Select **three** of the following towns:-Brisitol, Nottingham, Dundee,
Belfast. Name the chief industries carried on in the towns selected, and
say what advantages each town enjoys for the particular industries.

SECTION B

4. How does Holland differ from Norway in relief, climate, occupations,
and distribution of population ?

5. Some parts of the north German plain have a density of population of
over 500 to the square mile; others less than 150. How do you explain
these differences

6. Show how physical features have affected the growth of ports in the
Mediterranean sea-board from Gibraltar to Genoa and how climatic
conditions have affected agriculture.

7. What are the main differences in climate between Arabia and
Malaya? How have these differences affected the occupations of the
people and the density of population?

8. What advantages does **either** India or Japan possess for the
development of manufacturing industries? Give an account of the
manufacturing industries of the country you choose.

9. The Chinese have been called 'farmers of forty centuries'. What
geographical factors make agriculture of such permanent importance in
China?

10. Choose **three** of the following, describe their positions and explain
why they are important:- the Grand Banks, the Sault-Ste-Marie (Soo)
Canals,the Hudson-Mohawk gap, the Panama Canal.

11. What and where is the Canadian Shield? What are (a) its advantages, *(b)* its disadvantages for Canada?

12. If you went by air from New York to San Francisco what main physical regions of the United States would you cross? Choose two of these regions and compare their relief and climate.

13. Write notes on two of the following subjects
(a) Egypt is the gift of the Nile.
(b) Minerals attract man to the most inhospitable countries.
(c) The Pacific Ocean is less important than the Atlantic Ocean.

OXFORD LOCAL EXAMINATIONS
SCHOOL CERTIFICATE
FRIDAY, JULY 11, 1941
TIME ALLOWED - 1 ½ Hours.
French. 1

[Write FRENCH 1 at the head of each sheet of your answers.]

1. Translate into French:-

    I had set out in the morning without taking my umbrella, for the sun was shining and there was not a cloud in the sky. About noon I noticed a dark patch *(tache f.)* on the horizon, but I paid no attention to it. Half an hour later it was no longer a patch but a great black mass. The wind began to whistle. My dog stood still with his tail between his legs. I was in the middle of a vast plain without a tree or a rock. It was already raining when at last I found a ditch. I got into it, but the dog refused to follow me. He remained on the bank and looked at me. I soon understood why he acted thus, for the water was flowing in the ditch. It was already a brook; in a few minutes the brook became a river which carried off my stick and the lunch I had brought with me.

  2. Write, in about fifteen lines (120 words) of French, the story depicted in the sketches overleaf, including such descriptive detail as you consider relevant.

[Correct your work carefully: gross grammatical errors will be heavily penalized. You will gain nothing by writing at excessive length. You are particularly warned against the introduction of irrelevant memorized matter or undue repetition.]

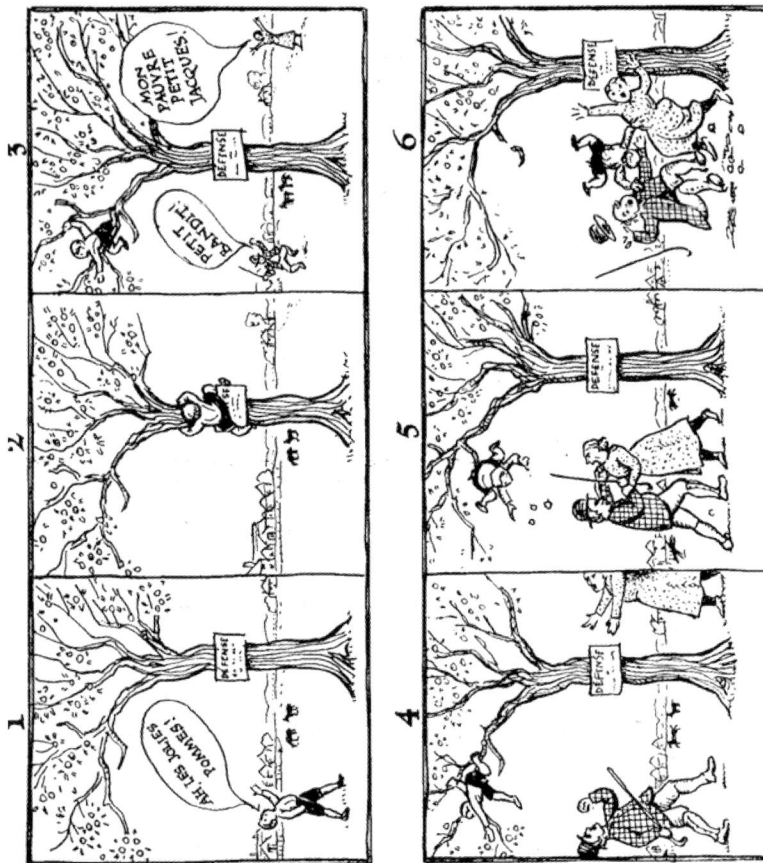

OXFORD LOCAL EXAMINATIONS
SCHOOL CERTIFICATE
FRIDAY, JULY 11, 1941
TIME ALLOWED- 1½ Hours.
French. II

[Write FRENCH II at the head of each sheet of your answers.]

Translate:

A warship in distress.

(a) Vers les sept heures du matin, nous entendîmes dans les bois un bruit de tambour: c'était le gouverneur, M. de La Bourdonnaye, qui arrivait à cheval suivi d'un détachement de soldats armés de fusils, et d'un grand nombre d'habitants. Il plaça ses soldats sur le rivage et leur ordonna de faire feu de. leurs armes tous à la fois. A peine eurent-ils tiré que nous aperçûmes sur la mer une lueur, et presque aussitôt un coup de canon retentit. Nous jugeâmes que le vaisseau était à peu de distance de nous, et nous courûmes tous du côte où nous avions vu son signal. Nous aperçûmes alors, à travers le brouillard, le corps et les vergues (yards) d'un grand vaisseau. Nous en étions si près que, malgré le bruit des flots, nous entendîmes les cris des matelots qui crièrent trois fois: Vive le Roi! car c'est le cri des Français dans les dangers extrêmes, ainsi que dans

grandes joies: comme si, dans les dangers, ils appelaient leur prince à leur secours, ou comme s'ils voulaient se déclarer prêts à périr pour lui.

My mothers diary

(b) Quand tout le monde était couché dans sa maison, que ses enfants dormaient dans leurs petits lits autour du sien, qu'on n'entendait plus que le, souffle régulier de leur respiration dans la chambre, le bruit du vent contre les volets *(Shutters)* les aboiements du chien dans la cour, ma mère ouvrait doucement la porte d'un cabinet rempli de livres; elle s'asseyait devant une petite table; elle prenait dans un tiroir quelques petits cahiers reliés en carton gris. Elle écrivait sur ces feuilles pendant une ou deux heures sans

relever la tête, sans hésiter pour choisir un mot ou une phrase, et sans que sa plume cessât un instant de courir sur le papier. C'était

l'histoire domestique de la journée qu'elle écrivaît. Ces notes ont fini par s'accumuler et par former, à sa mort, un précieux trésor de souvenirs pour ses enfants. Il y en a vingt-deux volumes.

2. **Read the following passage carefully, and answer, in English, the questions set upon it.** (No credit will be given for anything written in French):

L'auberge où nous descendîmes était dépourvue de provisions; trois diligences et deux chaises de poste avaient passé, et, semblables aux sauterelles (locusts) d'Égypte, les voyageurs avaient tout dévoré.
Ainsi disait le chef.
Cependant je voyais tourner une broche (spit) chargée d'un gigot tout à fait comme il faut, et sur lequel mes compagnes jetaient des regards significatifs.
Mais, hélas! le gigot appartenait à trois Anglais qui l'avaient apporté, et l'attendaient sans impatience en buvant du champagne. 'Mais du moins, dis-je d'un air moitié fâché et moitie suppliant, ne, pourriez-vous pas nous brouiller (scramble) des oeufs dans le jus de ce gigot? avec ces oeufs et une tasse de café à la crême nous nous contenterons.
- Oh! très volontiers, répondit le chef; le jus nous appartient de droit, et je vais tout de suite faire votre affaire.' Sur quoi il se mit à casser les oeufs avec précaution.
Quand je le vis occupé, je m'approchai du feu, et tirant de ma poche un couteau de voyage, je fis au gigot défendu une douzaine de profondes blessures, par lesquels le jus s'écoula jusqu'à la dernière goutte.

(a) What reason did the chef give for the lack of food at the inn?

(b) Why were the travellers not allowed to eat the joint which they saw roasting on the spit?

(c) What solution of the difficulty did the traveller propose ?

(d) What did the traveller do while the chef was busy ?

SCHOOL CERTIFICATE

WEDNESDAY, JULY 16, 1941

TIME ALLOWED-1 ½ Hours

Arithmetic

[All necessary work must be shown. No credit will be given for answers without sufficient work.]

Algebraical methods may be used, but NOT *Mathematical Tables.*

1. Simplify

$$\frac{1\frac{1}{7}+2\frac{7}{8}}{1\frac{3}{5}} \div (5\frac{1}{7} \times 6\frac{1}{4}),$$

Giving your answer in its lowest terms.

2. Evaluate as a decimal $\dfrac{0.\,0207 \times 0.752}{0.00368}$

3. A merchant buys butter at £9. 6s. 8d. per cwt. At what price per lb. should he sell it so as to make a profit of 12 ½ per cent. on his outlay?

4. Find, to the nearest penny, the difference between the Compound Interest and the Simple Interest on £3,450 for 3 years at 3 per cent. per annum.

5. A map is made to a scale of 1/25,000, i.e. one unit of length on the map represents 25,000 such units on the ground.
   Calculate (i) the actual distance in miles between two points represented on the map as 33.6 cm. apart;
   (ii) the actual area in square miles of a wood represented on the map as occupying an area of 16 sq. cm.
   [Take 1 kilometre = 0.622 miles and give your answers correct to three significant figures.]

6. A cubic foot of copper weighs 540 pounds. Find in grammes, correct to two decimal places, the weight of 1 cubic centimetre of copper, taking 1 pound = 0.453 kilograms and 1 cubic inch = 16.4 cubic centimetres.

7: Three partners, A, B, and C entering business, invest £2,500, £3600, and £4,700 respectively as capital.

From the profits in each year £450 is paid to A as manager's salary, and Income Tax at 7s. 6d. in the £ is deducted from the remainder. What is left is then divided amongst A, B, and C in proportion to the capital they have invested. Find the profits in a year in which A receives a total sum of £637. 10s.

8. Two motorists, P and Q, start together to drive their cars at constant speeds round a racing track 3¼. miles long. When P has completed the first circuit Q is 1,144 yards behind him. Find the ratio of their speeds.

When driving round the track in opposite directions at the same speeds as before they meet each other at intervals of 50 seconds.
What are their actual speed's in miles per hour?

OXFORD LOCAL EXAMINATIONS

SCHOOL CERTIFICATE

TUESDAY, JULY 15, 1941

TIME ALLOWED-2¼ Hours

Geometry

[No credit will be given for any attempt at a question in Practical Geometry if any of the construction lines are erased, and, when parallels or perpendiculars are drawn, the method used must be stated.

The use of a straight edge or compasses must in all cases be indicated by a drawn straight line or arc, that is, any constructed point must be shown as the intersection of two lines, not as a dot on one line.

It is unnecessary to draw very exact figures except in questions 5 and 7.]

Mathematical Tables may NOT *be used.*

1. Prove that an exterior angle of a triangle is equal to the sum of the two interior and opposite angles.

S, B, C, and T are four points in order on a straight line. The circle whose centre is B and radius BS meets the circle whose centre is C and radius CT in A. Prove that the angle SAT is obtuse.

2. Prove that the square on the hypotenuse of a right-angled triangle is equal to the sum of the squares on the other two sides.

If P is any point on the perpendicular drawn from the vertex *A* of the triangle ABC to the opposite side, prove that

$$PB^2 - PC^2 = AB^2 - AC^2$$

3. *AB* is a gven straight line. It is required to find a point P in *AB* produced either way such that the rectangle contained by *PA* and *PB* is equal to the square of a given length *l*. Show that P *may* be found ,in the following manner.

At A erect a perpendicular to AB and measure along it a length *AK* equal to *l*. Find 0 the middle point of AB. With 0 as centre and OK as radius describe a circle. Either intersection of this circle with *AB* is a position of P.

4. Show that, if a straight line touches a circle and from the point of contact a chord is drawn, the angles which this chord makes with the tangent are equal to the angles in the alternate segments.

Two circles intersect at, the points A and B. The tangent at A to the first circle meets the second circle at Q and the tangent at A to the second circle meets the first circle at P. A straight line drawn through A in any direction meets the first circle at S and the second circle at T. PS, and QT meet at K. Show that *SK = TK*.

[Only TWO of Questions 5, 6, 7 are to be attempted.]

5. Construct a triangle *ABC* from the following data. The side BC is 4.5 inches, the angle *ABC* is 40° and the radius of the inscribed circle is 1 inch.

Explain and justify your construction and measure the other sides and angles of the triangle.

6. Prove that, if two triangles are equiangular, their corresponding sides are proportional.

ABC is a plane triangle. A circle is drawn through A and C to touch BC at C and the tangent at C to the circle circumscribed about ABC meets the first circle at D. Prove that the triangles *ABC* and ACD are similar and that AC² = AB.*AD*.

7. The horizontal base ABC of a pyramid is an equilateral triangle. Its vertex V is vertically above the centre of the circle circumscribed about *ABC* and at a height above it equal to twice BC. Determine by geometrical constructions (i) the inclination of the edge VA to the horizontal, (ii) the inclination of the face VBC to the horizontal.

(Explain your figures and show clearly how your results are obtained.)

OXFORD LOCAL EXAMINATIONS
SCHOOL CERTIFICATE
FRIDAY, JULY 18, 1941
TIME ALLOWED - 1 ¾ Hours.

Algebra

[All necessary work must be shown. No credit will be given for answers without sufficient work.]

Each Candidate will be supplied with Mathematical Tables and one *piece of squared paper.*

1. In a school there are a pupils of whom *x* are boys and the rest girls. On a certain morning p per cent. of the boys and 2p per cent. of the girls are absent. Find an expression for the total number present.

2. Solve the equations

$$\tfrac{1}{3}(x-y) - \tfrac{1}{2}(x+2y) = 1, \qquad \tfrac{1}{3}(2x+y) - \tfrac{1}{2}(x+y) = 2.$$

(ii) Solve the equation

$$x^2 - 4x + 1 = 0$$

giving the roots correct to two places of decimals.

12

3. The value of the expression

$$\frac{ax^2 + 1}{bx}$$

is $2\frac{1}{2}$ when $x = 2$, and is $4\frac{3}{4}$ when $x = 4$.
Find the values of a and *b*.

4 Factorize

(i) $3x^2 - 2x - 8$ (ii) $a^6 - b^6$, (iii) $a(x-1)^2 - x(a-1)^2$.

5. If $u = x + \frac{1}{y}$ and $v = y + \frac{1}{x}$ prove that

$$u+v = (x+y)\left(1+\frac{1}{xy}\right) \quad \text{and}$$

$$\frac{(u+v)^2}{uv} = \frac{(x+y)^2}{xy}$$

6. Draw the graph of

$$y = 2\left(x + \frac{9}{x} - 8\right)$$

between the values $x = 1$ and $x = 8$, taking the side of one large square to represent 1 unit along each axis.
Find from your graph the range of positive values of x for which

$$x + \frac{9}{x} \text{ is less than 8.}$$

Find also a second value of *x,* for which y has the same value as when $x = 2.$ 1.

7. Solve the equations:

$$x^2 - 4y^2 - 2xy = 9$$
$$x - 2y = 6$$

8..Show that the sum of the first n terms of the geometrical progression   a+ar+ar² ... is

$$\frac{a(r^n - 1)}{r - 1}$$

Use logarithms to find the sum of the first 10 terms of the geometrical progression whose first term is 6.5 and whose common ratio is 1.65.

9. A dealer paid £56. 5s. in all for a number of articles. He sells them all at £4 each and thus makes a total profit equal to the price he paid for each article. How many articles did he buy?

OXFORD LOCAL EXAMINATIONS
SCHOOL CERTIFICATE
TUESDAY, JULY 22, 1941
TIME ALLOWED- 2 Hours
Trigonometry and Mensuration

[Write **TRIGONOMETRY** at the head of each sheet of your answers. The answers must be obtained by calculation, not by drawing and measurement. Tables of four-figure logarithms will be provided, and a corresponding degree of accuracy will be expected.
N.B-The full working must be shown.]

1. An aeroplane dives at the rate of 250 miles per hour in a direction making an angle of 40' with the horizontal. An observer on the ground first sees it at an angle of elevation of 70° and ten seconds later it is immediately overhead. What is its height, in feet, above the ground at the latter time ?

2. *ABCD* is a parallelogram in which $AB = 5$ inches, $BC = 10$ inches, and the diagonal *BD* is at right angles to *AB*. Calculate the acute angle between the diagonals and the length of the diagonal AC.

3. Two sides of a triangle are 15 and 22 inches long and the angle included between them is 37 °. Calculate the area of the triangle and the angle opposite the longest side.

4. A solid sphere of lead is melted down and recast in the form of a solid cone whose semi-vertical angle is 22°. Find what percentage of the surface of the original sphere the total surface area of the cone is.

5. *A, B* are two observation stations 3,000 yards apart and *B* is East of *A*. *D* is a point 2,500 yards South of *B*. An object C is observed from *A* on a bearing 37° East of North and from *B* on a bearing 25° West of North. If *ABCD* are all on the same level, calculate the bearing of C from *D*.

6. *ABC* is an equilateral triangle lying in a horizontal plane and its sides are 18 feet long. P is a point above the plane. The distances PA, PB are each 18 feet and the distance PC is 16 feet. Calculate the height of P above the horizontal plane.

OXFORD LOCAL EXAMINATIONS
SCHOOL CERTIFICATE
MONDAY, JULY 14, 1941
TIME ALLOWED-1 ¾ HOURS
Theoretical Chemistry. Paper I

[Write <u>THEORETICAL CHEMISTRY 1</u> at the head of each sheet of your answers.

Answer FIVE questions and no more. Answers should be illustrated by clear diagrams, and equations should be given wherever possible.]

1. State clearly the essential difference between a chemical and a physical change.

If a piece of sodium be placed in water it gradually gets smaller and presently disappears. So does a piece of salt. Point out what important differences there are between the two cases and quote **three** experiments by which you could demonstrate them.

2. State the law of multiple proportions.
An element E forms two oxides, containing 77.78 and 70.0 per cent. of E respectively.
(a) Calculate the two equivalent weights of E and show that they illustrate the above law.
(b) Assuming that the former oxide has the formula EO, calculate the atomic weight of E and write the formula of the latter oxide.

3. A mixture of 100 c.c. of hydrogen and 40 c.c. of oxygen was exploded in an eudionieter. After explosion the temperature was raised to 110° C. and the corrected volume of gases left was 100 c.c.. On cooling to room temperature the corrected volume became 20 c.c. This gas was hydrogen.

[**ALL** the above volumes are reduced to S.T.P.]

Calculate the composition by volume of (a) the hot gases after explosion, (b) the same after cooling.
State what this experiment tells you about the molecule of oxygen.
Sketch the apparatus in which the experiment could be carried out.

4. How would you prepare and collect a sample of nitrous oxide ?
Give **three** tests, with the results you would expect to obtain, by which nitrous oxide can be distinguished from oxygen.

5 Describe carefully how you would convert a sample of calcium hydroxide into bleaching powder.
What is the reaction of a filtered solution of bleaching powder with (a) an acidified solution of potassium iodide, *(b)* freshly precipitated lead hydroxide, (c) dilute sulphuric acid?

6. It is stated that when oxalic acid is heated with concentrated sulphuric acid, equal volumes of carbon monoxide and carbon dioxide are evolved. Describe, with sketches, how you would obtain each of these gases in a state of reasonable purity.
Briefly indicate how you would determine the percentage by volume of each gas in the mixture.

7. If you were given some sulphur and any other necessary chemicals and apparatus, how would you obtain and collect a quantity of hydrogen sulphide ?
What happens when hydrogen sulphide is (a) burnt in air, *(b)* dissolved in water and exposed to air, (c) passed into a solution of copper sulphate ?

8.How would you distinguish between the following pairs of substances ? (Give **two** tests for each pair, and state the results you would expect to obtain in each case.)
(a) Cupric oxide and manganese dioxide, (b) sodium carbonate and sodium bicarbonate, (c) permanently hard water and temporarily hard water, (d) a solution of sulphurous acid and a solution of chlorine in water.

Practical Chemistry. (B Paper)

[Write <u>**PRACTICAL CHEMISTRY B**</u> at the head of each sheet of your answers.
<u>State on your papers all letters and numbers marked on any envelope containing substances supplied to you.</u>]

Candidates should remember that the Examiner will form his judgement of their work from the description which he receives. It is therefore necessary to describe each experiment shortly but clearly.

Credit will be given for good methodical work, even if incomplete results are obtained. No credit will be given for a mere statement of results.

[H = 1, 0 = 16, S = 32]

1. The solution **N** contains 12 grams of sulphuric acid per litre. You are required to find the weight of the alkaline substance **P** which will neutralize 49 grams of sulphuric acid.

Weigh out about 2 grams of **P** for a 100 c.c. flask, or 5 grams for a 250 c.c. flask. Dissolve it in water, make up and titrate measured portions of the solution with the acid **N**, which should be in the burette. Use methyl orange as indicator.

2. Carry out the following experiments with substance **R**:-

(a.) Heat a portion in a dry tube and identify the gas given off. Describe the residue left in the tube.

(b) Treat a portion with dilute hydrochloric acid and identify the gas given off.

(c) To separate portions of the solution obtained in (b) add (i) sodium hydroxide solution gradually till in slight excess and heat the resulting solution carefully till no further change is apparent, (ii) ammonium hydroxide solution gradually till in considerable excess.

Describe what you observe in these experiments and draw conclusions as to the nature of **R**.

[Not more than FIVE questions are to be answered; of these, at least TWO MUST BE from the section on Mechanics.
Answers should be illustrated by diagrams, wherever possible.]

[Mathematical Tables will be provided.]

Mechanics

1. State *Boyle's Law,* and describe an experiment to test its truth.

A vessel has a volume of 2 litres, and air is forced into it by means of a pump whose volume is 140 c.c. How many strokes of the pump will be needed to raise the pressure in the vessel from one atmosphere to 2.4 atmospheres?

2. State *Archimedes' Principle,* and describe how you would verify it for the case of a floating body.

A body floats in oil of specific gravity 0.9 with five-sixths of its volume immersed. What fraction of its volume would be immersed if it were placed in water? Find the specific gravity of a liquid in which it will float with one ninth of its volume above the surface.

3. What do you understand by the *mechanical advantage, velocity ratio,* and *efficiency* of a machine ?

Draw a diagram of a pulley system with velocityratio of 5, and find the greatest load that a 12-stone man could raise with the aid of this machine if its efficiency is 60 per cent.

4. State the *parallelogram of forces* rule, and describe an experiment to test it.

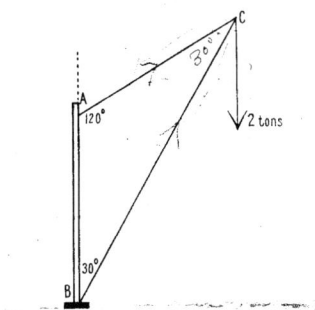

The figure represents a jib-crane, in which *AB is* the vertical post, BC the jib, and AC the tie. A load of 2 tons hangs from C. Find the forces in the jib and the tie.

Heat and Light

5. Define the terms *calorie* and *specific heat.*

Electric immersion heaters about the size of a table-spoon are used by placing them inside the liquid to be heated. Describe how you would find experimentally the number of calories produced per minute by such a heater.
Make a list of the likely sources of error, and explain how you would avoid each as far as possible.

6. What do you understand by the *apparent coefficient of expansion* of a liquid?

Describe how you would determine the apparent coefficient of expansion of alcohol, and explain how you would work out the result from your readings.
How does the expansion of water differ from that of most other liquids ?

7. Describe fully how you would project a pure *spectrum,* on a screen, using a source of white light.

Describe and explain what you would observe on the screen (a) if a piece of red glass were placed in the path of the light from the source, *(b)* if a piece of green glass were held over the red glass in the path of the beam, (c) if a sodium lamp were used instead of white light as the source.

8. Explain the term *refractive index,* illustrating your explanation by a diagram.

Give an account of some method of finding the refractive index of a liquid.

A ray of light strikes one face of a 60° glass prism used in the usual way at an angle of incidence of 50°. Trace the path of the ray through the prism, and find the angle of deviation. The refractive index of glass is 1.5.

(9) Describe experiments to show *(a)* that water is a bad conductor of heat, *(b)* that copper is a better conductor of heat than iron, (c) that a blackened surface absorbs radiant heat better than a polished one.

Magnetism and Electricity

10. What do you understand by a *neutral point?*

Describe how you would find the position of the neutral points which occur when a magnet is laid horizontally in the magnetic meridian with the S.-pole pointing northwards, and indicate the position of these points in a diagram.

The neutral points obtained when a short magnetis used for this experiment are found to be 20 cm. From the middle of the magnet. Calculate the magnetic moment of themagnet, given that H is 0.2 dynes per unit pole.

11. Give a detailed description of **either** the Daniell or the Leclanche cell.

What do you understand by the *electromotive force* of a cell?

When the upper fixed point of a thermometer is being tested accurately, care is taken (i) to have the thermometer bulb in the steam from boiling water, and not in the water itself, (ii) to find the pressure of the atmosphere at the time of the test. Explain as fully as you can the reason for these two precautions.

7. Explain the terms *intensity of illumination, illuminating power, foot candle.*

A man who has been using a 100candle-power lamp 4 feet above his desk replaces it by a 40 candle-power lamp 2 feet lower down. Calculate the change in the intensity of illumination at the level of the desk.

8. What do you understand by the focal *length of a concave mirror?* Deduce a formula connecting the distances of object and image and the radius of curvature of such a mirror.

An object is placed upright on the axis of a concave mirror, whose radius of curvature is 20 cm., at a distance of 5 cm. from the pole of the mirror.

Determine, graphically or otherwise, the magnification, position, and nature of the image formed by the mirror.

9. Explain how two lenses may be used to make a *compound microscope.* Draw a clear diagram tracing the paths of two rays through the instrument, the rays to be taken as coming from a point on the object which is not on the axis of the instrument.

Magnetism and Electricity

10. What do you understand by *(a) the magnetic meridian, (b) the dip,* at any given place ?

Describe the *dip-circle,* and explain how you would use it to determine the dip.
State what is observed while the instrument makes a complete revolution about a vertical axis.

11. Describe, and give a good diagram of the construction of, **either** *(a)* an induction coil, or (b) a simple dynamo. Explain how the apparatus works.

12. How would you find the *reduction factor of a* tangent galvanometer experimentally?

A tangent galvanometer has three sets of windings with 5, 20, and 50 turns respectively, all of the same radius. A current of 0.1 ampere gives a deflexion of 45° with the 20-turn coil. What will be the deflexion observed when the same current passes through *(a)* the 5-turn, (b) the 50-turn winding ?

13. What do you understand by the terms *electric potential, dielectric constant?*

How would you test experimentally whether the potential of an irregularly shaped insulated charged conductor was the same at all points of the surface ?
Calculate the force between two positive electric charges of 50 and 60 units placed 10 cm. apart in a medium of dielectric constant 6.